HIT ME
WITH YOUR BEST
SHOT

A FIGHT PLAN FOR DEALING
WITH ALL OF LIFE'S HARD KNOCKS

HIT ME
WITH YOUR BEST
SHOT

A FIGHT PLAN FOR DEALING
WITH ALL OF LIFE'S HARD KNOCKS

Revised Edition

Jackie Kallen

To Senita —
Jackie Kallen

PENMARIN BOOKS

Editorial Offices:	*Sales and Customer Service Offices:*
Penmarin Books	Midpoint Trade Books
1044 Magnolia Way	27 W. 20th Street, Suite 1102
Roseville, CA 95661	New York, NY 10011
(916) 771-5869	(212) 727-0190

Penmarin books are available at special discounts for bulk purchases for premiums, sales promotions, or education. For details, visit www.penmarin.com or contact the publisher. On your letterhead, include information concerning the intended use of the books and how many you wish to purchase.

Visit our Website at www.penmarin.com for more information about this and other exciting titles.

Printed in the United States of America
1 2 3 4 5 6 7 8 9 10 07 06 05 04 03

ISBN: 1-883955-33-5

Library of Congress Control Number: 2003109551

THIS BOOK IS DEDICATED TO

My supportive and loving sons, BRYAN and BRAD,

Their truly wonderful wives, STEPHENIE and MOLLY,

And my beloved grandsons, CHASE and BRYCE KALLEN.

Contents

Foreword

I met Jackie Kallen when I was a twenty-year-old, four-round fighter. From the first time we met, she took charge, organizing my life and helping me shape my career. She handled my publicity, both professionally and creatively, and she also shopped with me for clothes, cars, houses, and furniture. She advised me, not just about boxing issues, but on all issues. She has a lot of energy and ideas, and always goes above and beyond the normal call of duty. She doesn't just give 100 percent to a situation, person, or relationship——she gives 110 percent.

When Jackie started managing her own boxers, a lot of people questioned whether a woman could make it in what had always been a man's game. But they didn't know Jackie the way I did—— and still do. I had no doubts that she'd be a success. She succeeds at anything she does because she works hard, has a real passion for her projects, and truly cares about people. To many of these young kids just starting out, Jackie's like a mom——someone who is tough, fair, and determined to see them do their very best. Her fighters are like a family to her.

One of her best qualities is her loyalty. Many people will be right there during the good times. When I won six world championship belts in my time, I had a lot of friends, but Jackie was always there for me win, lose, or draw. After a crushing defeat, when the dust settled Jackie was there with a hug and a personal letter of love and support. She stands out for having a big heart in a rough business.

Jackie Kallen has been a very special person in my life. She has always been around when I need a shoulder to cry on or someone to talk to. I know I can always call her if I need something. She has been a problem-solver for me, so I'm sure her book will do the same for anyone who also aspires to be a world champion in whatever field he or she chooses. Whether it's business, sports, parenthood, or anything else, Jackie's book will help you to be the best you can be.

We've been friends for almost twenty-five years now, and I know our friendship will be everlasting. She's a great person to have on your team, too, so I know you'll love her book.

THOMAS "HIT MAN" HEARNS

Preface

Known as "The First Lady of Boxing," I have made my mark in the predominantly male field of boxing. This sport has taught me many important life lessons. We all face fights on a daily basis, and there are specific traits that all champions possess. That is what separates the winners from the losers. My years in the boxing world taught me that life is, indeed, like a fight. From birth to death, we are always fighting against something or someone. Studying and working with boxers for over two decades has shown me how many parallels there are between their life and ours.

When I wrote the first edition of this book in 1997, I was going through a really trying period in my life. My beloved mother had recently died, my husband of thirty years had divorced me, my father had suffered an irreversible stroke, and I had recently moved from the Detroit area to Los Angeles. I was reeling from all the changes in my life and was trying to make sense of it all. Writing this book was both cathartic and therapeutic. As I discovered, change can be a good thing, and I grew from my experiences because they actually made me a stronger, more resilient person.

I have since dealt with serious health issues such as two breast lumpectomies, a stent implant in my left artery, and the onset of menopause. These were small battles, easily overcome with a positive attitude, a ready smile, the right people around me, and preparation.

I learned the importance of taking charge of your own life and your own health. Your health is so important. Get annual checkups. Women, do breast self-examinations, get mammograms, and go for a bone-density test. These are simple procedures that can save your life. I have mild osteoporosis and take medication for it. I would never have known had I not gotten a simple bone-density test. And ask your doctor to give you a stress test. It's as simple as walking on a treadmill, and it can alert doctors if you have a heart condition. Don't wait for symptoms to surface to learn that you have a problem. Stay ahead of the game. Be proactive. This applies to men *and* women both.

Think of yourself as a major corporation. You are the CEO and make all the decisions. Run this company to be successful and productive.

Now, six years later, things could not be better. My life has inspired the Paramount Pictures film *Against the Ropes,* starring Meg Ryan, and I travel all over the country as a keynote speaker. My family is thriving, my health is great, I still manage boxers, and I am working on TV and radio projects. I have learned that the fight is never over until the final bell.

Acknowledgments

Hit Me With Your Best Shot was inspired by my late mother, Marjorie Cooper Kaplan Mahoney, who was as motivational a role model as any woman could have had.

Special thanks go to my late father, Phil Kaplan, who showed me that laughter is the best medicine, and my brother, Skip Kaplan, who is my best friend.

I want to acknowledge the following people for their guidance, belief, and encouragement:

> Andy Roth—The most dynamic speaking agent on the planet
> Hayden Meyer—Boy Wonder
> Stephen Breimer—An attorney worth liking
> Hal Lockwood and the gang at Penmarin—Wonderful people to work with
> Judye Kanfer—Men come and go, but a true girlfriend is a lifetime gift
> Gary Baldassarre—The man in my life, a real soulmate

And for those special people in my life who have been in my corner when I needed them most: You know who you are, and you know how much you mean to me

None of this would have been possible if I hadn't met a supremely talented young boxer in 1978 named Thomas Hearns and his manager/trainer Emanuel Steward. Working with them for all these years has been an education and an example of how much friendship counts in this day and age. I have learned that boxing is a microcosm of life itself. We all face opposition daily. It is how we deal with the challenges that determines the outcome.

About the Author

JACKIE KALLEN is a former journalist, television newscaster, and public relations consultant. She stands out not only as the most successful female boxing manager in the sport's history, but the first female to own and run her own boxing gym—Galaxy Boxing, in Detroit, Michigan. She formerly served as the first female commissioner of the International Female Boxing Association (IFBA) and was inducted into the Michigan Jewish Sports Hall of Fame. She travels the country as a keynote speaker, addressing corporate, university, and general audiences on success in the face of adversity, the topic of her book. The movie *Against the Ropes* was inspired by Jackie's remarkable life. Originally from the Detroit area, Jackie now lives in Los Angeles.

HIT ME WITH YOUR BEST SHOT

A FIGHT PLAN FOR DEALING
WITH ALL OF LIFE'S HARD KNOCKS

ROUND

1

BE PREPARED

Women today not only have to compete head to head with men on a daily basis, but they had better win more often than they lose or they won't be in the game long. It doesn't matter what the game happens to be, competition today is fierce, and the challenges bigger than ever. Giving 100 percent is no longer a goal but a necessity.

Being able to give it, though, requires more than just hard work or natural talent. To be the best you must combine your own natural abilities with hard work—in a way that will allow you to attain the best possible results.

Competition brings out the best in all of us. Yet we rarely talk about what specific traits set a champion apart from the rest of the pack. I believe the qualities that make a great fighter are the same ones that make a great executive, a great teacher, a great lover, or a great friend. The losers in life may attribute the success of others to luck, but the winners know better.

There are three key elements that are absolutely essential for a boxer to be a champion. The first is *natural ability*. In boxing, this means natural coordination, speed, timing, and instinct. Having natural ability means knowing when to make the right moves and how to fight a smart fight. Outside the ring, this could mean natural sales ability or a natural artistic aptitude. It could be a talent for working with numbers or computers. It could be a flair for organizing or cooking. It is the God-given talent that each of us possesses.

The second element I look for in a fighter is what's called *heart*. This is harder to define. It's determination and drive, of course, but also a willingness to sacrifice, before and during the big fight, to come out a winner. I don't care if someone is the best "technically sound" fighter in the world. If he has no heart, then he will never be a world-class champion. Heart is that quality that gives him the drive, motivation, courage, and will to go the distance to get what he wants. If someone doesn't have determination and perseverance he will not succeed. It's just that simple. Natural talent will only take a person so far. I'd take a fighter who

2

has heart and little talent over a fighter who has talent but no heart. You can always teach someone to fight, but you cannot teach him to have heart. I've seen fighters with great natural ability fail, and just average boxers make it to the top. Winning comes from within.

The third key element of a winner is his *training habits* and the lifestyle he chooses for himself. If he does drugs, doesn't listen to advice from the trainers and managers, or is just plain sloppy in his preparation for a fight, then he not only can't win, he doesn't deserve to win. This applies to life outside the ring as well. Lifestyles and choices contribute greatly to a person's success or failure.

Talent, heart, and the right training habits are the essential basic attributes that every manager and trainer looks for in a fighter. These are the same attributes that a boss should look for in an employee. But, even more important, they are the qualities we should all look for and try to develop in ourselves. If any one of these attributes is missing, then you will never be a champion.

As I've learned, there is no easy way to the top—no shortcut to the championship. If you're looking for an easy route to success, then this is not the book for you. To be a great boxer, teacher, business executive, or life partner takes hard work. Championship fights often last less than an hour, but that short span of time is fueled by a lot of preparation. The difference between a champion and a contender is almost always in the preparation. A champion prepares to win through hard work and smart training. A loser prepares to lose by either not working hard enough or not taking the fight seriously enough.

Think of this book as a training camp for your life. Some chapters may remind you of commonsense practices that you might have neglected or forgotten along the way. All of us need to be reminded of the basics from time to time. Throughout I've incorporated boxing metaphors that I've recognized as valuable and have adopted in my own life and business. Although this book is not a shortcut, it is everything I know about winning.

What's a Nice Girl Like Me Doing in a Sport Like This?

That's a question I've been asked thousands of times. I was working as an entertainment and sports writer for a daily newspaper in the Detroit area. I was assigned an interview with a young fighter named Thomas Hearns. I wrote the story, watched him fight, and fell in love with the sport. In the nearly fifteen years since I began managing professional fighters, I've managed a stable of boxers that included world champions and serious contenders; I've negotiated multimillion-dollar television deals; and I've built my own gym. And I did it on my own terms and in my own style. This is not only true of my work in boxing, but of everything I've done. As a journalist, television newscaster, and public relations consultant with my own agency, I've done things my own way. Perhaps that's why I have an affinity for boxing.

Boxing is the apex of sport. Ironically, it is also the most basic of sports. No space-age plastics protect the participants as they do in football or hockey. There is a minimum of equipment and rules, and it can often be a raw and brutal sport. As for the fighter, he is the ultimate individualist. Being a great fighter requires a strong sense of self-worth and an unshakable confidence in the abilities he's worked so hard to develop. Each time a fighter enters the ring to face an opponent, he has to be in the best shape of his life, both physically and mentally. The best boxers—the ones who make it to the top—fight each match as if it were for the title.

Does that philosophy remind you of anything? It should, because boxing is exactly like life. Your opponent may not be a 240-pound heavyweight like Lennox Lewis. He or she may be a boss, coworker, client, spouse, lover, or friend. The conflict may be a single three-minute round or a twelve-round championship bout. People encounter conflicts every day, and the way they deal with them determines the outcome of their careers and relationships.

A professional fight is more than punching an opponent until he falls down and the ref counts to ten. A fight is also a test of natural ability, strategy, and most of all, preparation. It's knowing how to avoid the low blows before they arrive, and having the skill to bob and weave around whatever else your opponent throws at you. It's a conflict with both rules and clearly defined winners and losers.

We would all like to eliminate the negative in our lives and focus on the positive. That's a wonderful goal, but unrealistic at best. We all have our share of stress and tension, regardless of gender. Years ago men were the punchers and fighters. Women were the ones who prettily bobbed and weaved their way around trouble. The men went out into the world, and the women spent their lives deflecting all of the bad that might come their way. And if things got really bad, well, the women could always call on the big, strong man to lend a hand. Those days are history. Regardless of whether you think that was a wonderful state of affairs or a complete catastrophe doesn't change the way things are now. The reality today is that it often takes two incomes for a family to meet its needs. Women have ventured out in the world and begun fighting their own battles. And, if anything, women have to fight harder and smarter than men. There are a lot of hard knocks out there. Women had better be ready to deal with them by knowing when to meet a challenge head-on, and when and how to roll with the punches. Women today have to learn how to punch with the big boys. Not accepting or preparing for the challenge is the best way I know of losing, and of making yourself a target. That's as true in life as it is in the ring.

When I first got into boxing, a well-known sportswriter told me the only women in boxing should be the "ring-card girls." They are the scantily dressed women who parade around the ring between rounds smiling and displaying cardboard signs announcing the round number. With all due respect to the ring-card girls, their job was not what I had in mind for myself. This particular writer wasn't voicing just his opinion: boxing was and is the ultimate boy's club. The cigar-chomping, tough-guy image of old movies is not terribly far from the truth. Talk about *macho*. The testosterone is so thick in the boxing world you can cut it with a knife. I had to overcome sexism and dodge rumors at every step. I had to fight to earn the respect of the boxers, managers, trainers, and promoters. I could not have faced tougher odds if I had put on a pair of gloves myself and gone ten rounds with Mike Tyson. What pulled me through, aside from determination, was preparation. From the very beginning, I entered every situation knowing as much if not more about boxing as a sport and an industry than anyone else there.

It also helped me to develop a thick skin. I learned not to pay much attention to idle gossip, and I never took myself too seriously. When one of my boxers won a close match, it was whispered that I must have paid off the judges. Instead of getting defensive and protesting, I merely laughed it off and moved on to the next fight.

If we look at famous winners—professional athletes, actors, successful business executives, and politicians—we realize that we put certain people up on pedestals. This happens to such a degree that their victories, both small and large, no longer surprise us. Indeed, their victories seem natural, inevitable, and deceptively effortless. "Of course they won," we think to ourselves, "they're *winners.*"

Often we classify people as winners and losers as if being a winner is an attribute one is born with, like black hair or blue eyes. Nothing could be further from the truth. Winning, more often than not, is the result of a series of specific steps that begins with training and ends with victory. Natural talent is part of it. So is hard work. And so is knowing what fights to accept. There are plenty of naturally talented athletes who never make it to professional status, and there are loads of hard workers who find themselves dead-ended in their careers or their personal lives—often not even realizing what they did "wrong."

Winning and losing are the end results of very different processes. Winning results from preparation, desire, talent, and discipline. Losing often results from laziness, lack of preparation, and indifference. In most of our lives, the difference between winning and losing is the way we go about the tasks in front of us. If the people we think of as winners have any advantage over their peers at all, it is that they have learned steps necessary to become a winner.

When we see someone win, we only see a small portion of the story. That victory did not just materialize out of thin air. It was designed, not destined. Just as an architect designs a building, winners design their victories. Just as a building needs a strong foundation, so too do our victories. It cannot be stressed too much: Training and preparation are major keys to success.

Training is a series of steps that include physical training, mental conditioning, and formulating a strategy. Champions not only train hard, they train smart. I will show you how all these elements work together to build a strong foundation for any challenge you take on.

Another key to success in boxing or any field is getting the right people in your corner. Just as a fighter's chances of winning can be determined by his trainer, manager, and others providing aid and strategy in his corner during the fight, our chances are improved by having the right people in our corners. These people are often our friends, family, and even coworkers. They should be selected, when possible, with the greatest care. You are judged by the people you surround yourself with, and these are the people who can affect your moods, your self-confidence, and your level of success.

No fighter steps into the ring without a fight plan, and no successful person takes on a task without first developing a strategy. In the following chapters I will guide you through the formulation of fight plans and strategy—and even provide guidelines to determine whether a particular fight is even worth accepting. After all, why take on a fight unless there is a good reason? Before going into battle, try to level the playing field as much as possible and whenever you can. Tip the odds in your favor!

Another quality that all champions have in common is attitude—an attitude of not only expecting to win, but deserving to win. This attitude is infectious. A winner knows he is good and revels in his victory. His confidence can be felt by everyone around him. His confidence in his abilities is not only established in his own mind but is accepted by everyone with whom he comes in contact. There is no secret to this. Self-confidence is not only something that is learned, it is also earned. I will show you just how to learn it and earn it.

Another element to leading a successful life is aggressiveness. You should pursue your career aggressively, love aggressively, and most of all, pursue happiness aggressively. Those who sit and wait timidly for the world to come to them will wait a very long time—without any real chance of winning. Passion is your number one tool. In order to be happy, successful, and fulfilled, you need to be passionate about the things that are important to you.

Of course, there is nothing wrong with sitting on the sidelines—if that is what you truly want to do. However, the vast majority of those who wait quietly would really like to get in there and "punch with the big boys" and show the world what they are capable of doing. For them, it's just a matter of being shown how to go about it. They need a nudge, some motivation, some incentive.

Then there are others who are overly aggressive. They are the ones who are always battling and chasing, first in one direction and then in another, often without any kind of plan at all. They are the ones who end up weary—often no further ahead than if they'd just sat on the sidelines. They may have the ambition and natural talent to be a champ, yet they never manage to focus their energies or even pick their fights carefully. This book will explain not only how to become more aggressive in pursuing those things that are important and worthwhile to you, but how to do it in the most efficient, conscientious ways possible.

Look at your life as a boxing match. We will cover various scenarios that are likely to occur in a boxing ring, and analogize them to those that we are likely to find in our personal and professional lives. These include recovering from "hard hits" that can leave us staggering; avoiding the low blows of a dishonest opponent; bobbing and weaving around trouble; accepting losses, knowing when to throw in the towel; and best of all, winning. What I hope to do in this book is to help set you on the right path to become the superstar in your own field of endeavor and, perhaps even more important, in your personal life.

There is absolutely no reason to hit another person outside of a ring. Boxing is a sport, and as such, the participants are bound by rules during their bouts. They are evenly matched by weight and ability. They are under the scrutiny of refs, judges, and the audience. It is these elements that transform boxing into a sport. It is in this sport, its training techniques, and a thorough appreciation for the hard work that goes into making a champion that the lessons in this book have their origins. I am not a fan of violence, and just because I love the sport of boxing does not mean that I advocate it in any form. Those who would attempt to solve their problems through violence are sadly misled. They will *not* solve even the smallest of their problems, and they will undoubtedly increase them instead. And any man who would raise his hand to a woman, child, or animal, even in the heat of anger, proves himself the worst kind of coward.

Training: The More You Sweat the Less You Bleed

There probably isn't a person in America today who hasn't seen the *Rocky* movies. Remember the first one, before all the Roman numerals began appearing? The hero, a down-and-out underdog, is picked by chance to take on the champ and eventually triumphs. If you watched the film carefully, you saw that the movie isn't just about the big fight at the end. Most of the story is about training. It's about Rocky getting ready for the fight. Every job or relationship you undertake should include Rocky-like preparation. He gained the respect and admiration of his friends as well as strangers when they saw how hard he trained.

If I told you that there was a fighter who stepped into the ring without training or preparation and got beat up, you wouldn't be surprised. Yet it amazes me how many people will go into an interview or start a job without preparation. Even more amazing is how they are genuinely surprised when they don't get the job or are immediately overwhelmed by the workload. With all the information available on the Internet, in the libraries, and from myriad other resources, there is no longer any excuse for lack of preparation.

If you have a big presentation for a major customer or client, prepare for it harder and longer than the competition. Do your homework. Research everything there is to know about the client and his or her products. Research the competition and discover their weaknesses before doing the presentation. Talk to people you know who may have worked at the company in the past. Go to the library and get the company's annual reports or other material, such as trade magazines. Find out all you can about the firm, their products, and the industry in which they compete. If you want the business, then train for winning it.

Once you're offered the job, keep on training. Find out before the first day what kind of computer programs they use. If it's a program you haven't used, then get the program and practice with it. Check out local colleges for night courses that may relate to the industry or job. Do everything you can to assure your own success. Never get complacent.

Before I ever sign a fighter, I've learned everything there is to know about that fighter, including his win-loss record as well as his reputation among trainers, other boxers, and promoters. I've studied his fight videos as carefully as any opponent to assure myself that he has what it takes to be a champion. And when I walk into a meeting with television executives, I've also done my homework. I've already researched the ratings and previous contracts of similar fights they may have broadcast. I know how many seats are in the arena and the size of the crowd we can expect to draw. When I am speaking to an audience, I have to prepare ahead of time. I need to know who these people are and how to slant my presentation.

During every professional match, what looks like several rounds of chaotic fighting in the ring is actually a lot of intensive training. Many fights are won or lost long before the boxers climb between the ropes and into the ring. The match itself often comes down to which of the opponents built on his natural talent and abilities by training harder and smarter. It's also about attitude. Who wants it the most?

Training also means sacrifice. A fighter who is "hungry" not only wants to win but is willing to make sacrifices in his own life in order to win. A boxer who shows up at the gym early every day and trains hard is training to win. He may not have had a single professional match, but he's preparing to be a winner. I can always spot this fighter. He's the one who is eating the right foods, avoiding alcohol, and following all the rules. He is the one who is willing to make sacrifices for what he wants because he wants success badly.

It's just as easy to spot the other kind of boxer. He's the one who will show up at the gym late in the afternoon hung over and then will go through the motions of training. He's traded a night of partying with his friends for a day of training. Neither one of these fighters may ever be champ, but which one has the better shot at the title? Which one has a better chance to grab an opportunity when it's presented? It isn't even a contest. Some say that there is no such thing as a lucky punch. A boxer either got lazy or his opponent got smart.

It's exactly the same situation in an office. The employee who consistently comes in late, leaves exactly at the stroke of five, and then goes home to sit in front of the television has little chance of success against someone who comes in early, works late, and prepares for each job as if it were a championship bout. Realistically, we live in uncertain times. Both employees may end up getting downsized and losing their jobs, but which one has a better chance of succeeding? Which one is in a better position to take even a small opportunity and build on it? Hard work is not a cliché. It is a path to victory.

In relationships the same principles apply. How many times have you heard happily married couples explain that they attribute their longevity to "hard work"? They have learned to work at their relationship each and every day. The man remembers birthdays and anniversaries. He brings home flowers and gifts for no reason. He goes to social events when he'd rather lie on the couch and watch TV. The wife cooks his favorite meals for him. She keeps her weight in check and tries to always look good. She doesn't nag. They make an effort to please each other, and they have learned to compromise.

Organization and preparation are key elements to training smart. The fighter who goes to the gym and works frantically at the wrong equipment or in a disorganized fashion may be training hard, but a lot of his effort is wasted. The fighter who "trains smart" will have a well-planned routine for each day. When he walks into the gym in the morning, he knows exactly what he has to accomplish that day. He realizes the clock is ticking down to his next fight, and he can't afford to waste a single day. He has to become as good as he can get, as quickly as possible.

Training is more than a matter of hard work. It also includes the right kind of hard work. It is absolutely crucial to remember that no two jobs or relationships are alike, just as no two fighters are alike. In the months leading up to a fight, a boxer will watch numerous hours of videos of his opponent. He'll study each of his opponent's bouts carefully. If the other fighter has a tendency to let his guard down on his right side, the smart boxer will not only make a note of this but practice hitting toward that side in preparation for his opponent's mistake. Each fighter has his own unique style. Some come out into the center of the ring slugging, while others rely more on footwork, moving around the ring, gracefully deflecting punches and looking for an opportunity. A smart boxer—a champ—will train differently for each opponent. This does not mean that he gives up his own unique style, but that he's able to adapt to different situations. The best fighters can adjust their fighting style to one that will be most effective against whatever opponent they face.

So the next time you are facing an opponent, take a moment to determine his or her personal style and react with that information in mind. Evaluate the other person's strengths and weaknesses. Discover which buttons to press to get the reaction you desire.

Now touch gloves and come out fighting!

GET THE RIGHT PEOPLE IN YOUR CORNER

One reason boxing is the ultimate sport is because the fighters compete one-on-one. It's just one person against another, and may the best one win. That's part of its irresistible appeal. However, when the bell rings and the boxer heads out into the center of the ring to face his opponent, he knows that his corner is there for him. Even as he takes those first steps under the lights, he is keenly aware that there are people behind him—literally and figuratively. He has a team supporting him who can be counted on to help him finish the fight by offering first aid, advice, support, and encouragement.

In this respect, boxing is very much a team sport. The fact that the team operates largely behind the scenes in no way diminishes their important contributions. Long before any of my boxers walks out into the ring to fight, he knows that not only am I behind him completely but that I've also assembled the best possible team in his corner. He has had the best trainers and facilities to prepare in, I have negotiated the best possible financial deal for him, and he has good lawyers at his disposal. He is prepared for the fight in the best possible manner.

The same principles apply to my life and my career. Professionally, I have a speaking agent, a talent agent, and an entertainment attorney. They are all part of my team. On the personal side I have my family, my man, and my friends behind me. Every positive moment in my life has been due—in part—to my team.

Do those things make a difference in the way a boxer fights? Certainly the trainers and facilities can make a huge impact on a fighter's performance in the ring. When a boxer is confident and satisfied with his corner, it allows him to enter the ring with a clear mind, completely focused on the job at hand. It is a matter of trust and confidence. When you trust the people around you, it increases your level of confidence.

It is a boxing truism that fights can be "won or lost in the corner." With each round typically lasting three minutes, with one minute of rest between, what happens in the corner between rounds is a quarter of the fight. Within that one minute, the fighter must get everything he needs to continue fighting to win.

That small space on the ring's apron is occupied by the trainer, his second, and the cut man. Once the end-of-the-round bell rings, they all must jump into action. They have just one minute to provide the fighter with ice water to cool him down, apply first aid, impart valuable fight advice, and wash out his mouthpiece so that, when the bell rings again at the end of those short sixty seconds, he can go back to the center of the ring not only feeling physically better but more confident than when he sat down.

The corner must function as a well-oiled machine, similar to a pit crew at the Indianapolis 500. In the heat of the moment, there is no time for petty squabbles or missteps. The sole focus of every member of a fighter's corner is the boxer and his needs. If it's a good corner, made up of smart professionals, they know exactly what their fighter will need and will have already prepared for it before the bell rings.

Everyone has a job to do, and he'd better do it to the best of his ability if he wants his fighter to win. Not only must the corner know the needs of the fighter and their own jobs, but they should also be aware of each other's activities in order to function smoothly. A good corner is a picture of efficiency, coordination, and expertise. As anyone in the fight business will tell you, apparent confusion or arguments in the corner between rounds is not a good sign. It reflects badly on the fighter's corner and management and on the fighter himself.

For example, when Mike Tyson lost his fight to Buster Douglas for the heavyweight title many years ago, it was widely reported that Tyson had a terrible corner. He was the world champion—perhaps one of the greatest fighters of the era—yet his own corner may have dragged him down. According to reports from the fight, the first-aid kit didn't include Enswell, a device especially designed to reduce inflammation around the eyes or cheeks during a fight. It is one of the most basic tools of any cut man in the sport. Instead, an old-fashioned rubber glove or condom filled with ice was used.

You may think that a fighter like Tyson, who more often than not disposes of his opponents in the first round, doesn't need a great corner and a full first-aid kit. He just has to walk out, punch, and walk back to collect his check. All that corner expertise is wasted because they rarely, if ever, have to leap into action. But nobody can or should try to do it alone—even a champion. And we all have a bad day now and then. Those are the times we must rely on our support system.

To succeed in anything, whether in boxing, business, or one's personal life, nobody can win the big fights entirely on his own. In my experience in the sports, business, and entertainment worlds, I have never met a successful man or woman who didn't have a great team behind him or her. Everyone has someone to thank and with whom he or she should share the credit. Picture yourself at an awards ceremony. You have just won a gold statuette for "Mother of the Year," "Teacher of the Year," or "World's Best Tennis Player." Who would you thank in your acceptance speech? Hopefully you won't have trouble coming up with your list of names.

When I began my business, I went to great lengths to assemble the best team possible in my corner, including bankers, lawyers, accountants, publicists, and secretaries. The same is true for any successful business. The multimillion-dollar deal is the result of the secretaries, assistants, and other staff members who supported the executive who signed the big client or made the big sale. The best executives recognize this fact and are only too happy to share the credit. The executive may be out canvassing and trading punches with the competition, but he is only as good as the people he has in his corner. Lazy, nonproductive people do not help and ultimately slow him down and lower the quality of his work. That's true for every level of an organization, from the CEO to the janitorial staff.

Just as a champ needs the best possible people in his corner, the best people need the proper tools to get the job done right. You can have a crackerjack support staff who excel in every possible way, but if all they have to work with are outdated computers, temperamental phone lines, and an inadequate photocopier, then they will never perform to their full potential. Any CEO of a major corporation would be significantly hindered by a staff working under less than optimum conditions.

I'm always amazed by the executive who spends thousands of dollars buying himself the latest streamlined laptop with all of the high-tech bells and whistles and then provides only the most basic computer system for his support staff. This not only creates hard feelings on the part of the staff, it lowers the quality of their work as they labor to make do with inadequate tools. This kind of behavior also sends the signal that their jobs aren't important to the success of the company or department. Consequently, they begin to feel that if their jobs aren't important and their contributions aren't vital, then what's the point of giving 100 percent every day?

One of the most important things you can develop in your corner is trust. The fighter who does not trust (or listen to) the between-rounds advice of his trainer is at a serious disadvantage. The trainer who doesn't trust the work or judgment of the cut man might make the wrong decisions in terms of offering advice, which can easily have repercussions down the chain of command. Trust is essential for any team to function efficiently and smoothly. This trust is built on expertise in the field and also on personal experience and mutual respect.

A good trainer, for instance, knows his fighter. He's been with him through other fights and understands not only his style but his limitations. He knows when to urge him to "go for the knockout," and when that advice might put too much pressure on the fighter or represent an impossible task.

The same is true in business. An executive who doesn't trust his or her support staff to get the job done, offer honest advice, and function as a team is at a serious disadvantage. Any energy that's expended in conflicts within a team is energy that isn't focused on the real opponents, such as a competing firm. It's just common sense, yet it's forgotten every day in the petty conflicts of office politics.

We can and should apply the same principles to our personal lives. We should never try to climb into the ring alone. Whenever we step into a ring, whether it be the boardroom or with a loved one, we need to know that someone we trust is behind us to offer comfort, support, and advice. We all need the right people in our corner. Friends, relatives, and spouses are the people who give us the things we need between rounds. Not only can they supply motivation and encouragement, they may know how to help us to perform our best.

Be careful when selecting your inner circle of friends. Choose people whose opinions you respect. Look for people who will be honest without being cruel, who are as quick to do a favor as to ask for one, and who not only talk the talk—they walk the walk. Would you seek romance advice from a friend who has been married four times before and is on her fifth divorce? Would you ask for business advice from a person who has gone broke twice and is currently unemployed?

Our teams are the people we love and those with whom we work. These are the people who share our lives. They are our support system; some of them function in a professional capacity, such as a doctor or lawyer, others are our friends and spouses. All too often, we don't realize just how valuable these relationships are to our lives. We take them for granted. This is wrong for two reasons. First, nobody likes to be taken for granted. That's just basic human nature. It's nice to be needed, but being appreciated is also important. Together they make the best combination. Second, we need to evaluate the contributions these people make to our lives.

I keep two mental lists in my mind. One is my list of people who I believe need me more than I need them. They often seek my advice, ask for my help, and need a shoulder to lean on. I am their mentor. The other list contains the names of the people who I feel I can turn to for advice, support, and nurturing. They are my mentors. In life we need both lists.

All of us should take a long, hard look at our support network of friends and coworkers from time to time and ask some difficult questions. Are these people a positive influence? Friends who accept and encourage us toward our goals can be one of the greatest assets in the world, but friends who offer the wrong advice or discouragement can prove fatal. Never ask a catty or jealous friend to tell you if something looks good on you. She will tell you that you look lousy when you look terrific, and she will let you go out in something that doesn't look great just so you won't look better than she does.

In the boxing world, I've seen good fighters ruined by bad relationships and the wrong friends. It is not uncommon in the sports world to find athletes surrounded by so-called friends or girlfriends who encourage them to break training by going out drinking or nightclubbing. Boxers are notorious for their entourages. The right relationship can be the best thing in the world for a boxer. A wife or girlfriend can offer comfort, encouragement, and constructive criticism, and can make the difference between becoming a good fighter or a champ. However, a bad relationship can destroy the whole team, bringing divisiveness and hostility where there should be teamwork and harmony.

I signed a fighter once who was a good prospect. He was married, which was a good sign, and had a stable home life. However, the minute he began his professional career, his wife became a source of dissension and conflict. She started fights with him at home. She demanded his attention nearly every waking hour. She competed for his time. Perhaps this was a form of jealousy or simply nervousness at his budding career. I still don't know. But eventually he got arrested for beating her up, and his career never developed. He could never focus.

Boxing is not an easy profession. It requires dedication and absolute attention on the part of the fighter. This fighter's wife should have known that and helped him to focus his attention on his training, rather than on herself. A good corner ideally has the same goal as the fighter: winning. When the boxer's goal differs from that of his family, the results are often disastrous.

The same holds true for friends. Friends who take a fighter's focus away from his training schedule and upcoming matches show that they care little for his career or his goals. I cannot tell you the number of times I've seen talented boxers with genuine promise destroyed by their so-called friends. Not surprisingly, these friendships tend to disappear just as the athlete's career begins to wane. No doubt these people move on to find their next "victim," leaving the athlete wondering what went wrong.

I am not suggesting that work should take priority over family, but a good supportive family and loyal friends can be valuable assets to anyone involved in a difficult endeavor. If family members and friends care about you, they will work with you to help you achieve your goals. This is true whether you are out in the ring or taking your turn in the corner. In truth, part of the blame in these situations can be assigned to the boxer. He may not have related to family and friends the time commitment or the depth of concentration that is involved.

The concept of building a solid team applies to every aspect of life. Most of us judge others by the company they keep. If you see a person hanging out with drug dealers, you will assume they also deal drugs. On the other hand, if you see a group of professionals at lunch, you will assume they are all gainfully employed and well educated. It is all a matter of perception.

Those closest to you should understand your goals and the way you intend to reach those goals. For instance, the executive working on a major presentation should share the details of the presentation, its probable outcome, and any changes in his work schedule with his family. The homemaker who plans to return to school for a degree should discuss the details of her plan, including scheduling, with her spouse and children. After all, it's going to affect all of them. On the surface this seems basic, yet it's often neglected.

These are all things you can control. You can choose your friends. You can decide where and with whom you work. And you can certainly choose your spouse. Every area of your life affects the other areas. The friends who keep you out late at night can certainly impact the quality of your work the next day. Having a moody coworker makes going to work an unpleasant chore and puts you in a foul mood when you return home to your family. It's important to create balance in your life.

Outside of the boxing world, we all play two roles. Sometimes we are the main event, and other times we act as cornermen for the people we love and care about. Each role is equally important. The most high-powered executive in the world shouldn't be too proud or busy to offer encouragement and advice to a spouse who may be dealing with problems in her career, with her children, or in other areas of life.

I know women who *always* seem to end up in relationships with the wrong type of man. Nine times out of ten, it's because they have the wrong friends in their corner. Inevitably, they frequent the wrong nightclubs, bars, and parties, and they receive bad advice on everything from clothing and hairstyles to dating and major life decisions. Their friends do not support them with the right advice, and they frequently steer them in entirely the wrong direction. Sometimes this is done out of disloyalty or jealousy. Other times the people in their corner are just not interested enough to voice an honest opinion. In other words, they just don't care.

Perhaps the most important aspect of this concept is knowing who is there for you and who isn't. A fighter can glance over his shoulder and see his corner behind him, grouped together just beyond the ropes. In life, however, it isn't that easy. It's difficult to identify true friends who have your best interests at heart. I often hear my own friends complain about how one of their supposedly good friends betrayed them.

One instance in particular stands out, when a friend of mine was having trouble with a teenage child. The teenager was staying out until all hours of the night, associating with a rough crowd, and was thought to be taking drugs. My friend was frantic with worry at not being able to control her child. She made the mistake of confiding in a coworker she thought was her friend. This woman had always been pleasant and willing to lend a hand when the work piled up, and they'd often gone out to lunch. When she heard the story, the woman was quite understanding and eager to offer sympathy to my friend. However, mere hours after she confided in this "friend," the story was all over the office. It became a source of gossip. And, as is the nature of gossip, the story of her teenager's wild ways was exaggerated with each telling. Eventually her boss found out, months after the teenager was making good progress in therapy and receiving better grades in school. By then the damage was done. My friend was turned down for a promotion because her boss thought she should be spending more time at home and focusing on her "drug addict" teenager.

The point of this story is twofold. First, rely on your corner—not virtual strangers or acquaintances—for support. Not only will the quality of advice be better, but you'll feel more comfortable in presenting them with a complete picture of any problem you may have. Second, choose the members of your corner wisely. We all want friends we can depend on and who feel they can depend on us. However, even the best of us sometimes find ourselves rushing into friendships with people who are neither trustworthy nor interested in reciprocating. Perhaps they hold some other appeal, such as being fun to go out on the town with. Such a reason, however, is not the way to choose people you want in your corner.

People select new friends for varying reasons, so be cautious about getting too close to someone right after meeting them. It's a good idea to enter a new friendship with both eyes open and give yourself time to evaluate the person and their agenda before opening up too much.

When we put someone in our corner, we should follow the same dictates that boxers do when they staff their corners. The people they choose have a history with them and have proven themselves in past fights. As a manager, when I look at a fighter's corner with the trainer, I look for the record of the fighters that the people in the corner have worked with previously. The fighter's wins are also their wins.

It pays to look around at your own group of friends every once in a while. If everyone in your group is moving from job to job, marriage to marriage, and crisis to crisis, maybe you should begin to change your friends. I'm not talking about ridding yourself of friends because they are experiencing a case of bad luck or have made a mistake. I am describing those people who live a life of constant problems, one after another, and who make no effort to turn their lives around.

A loser is someone who makes the same mistake over and over again but keeps expecting a different result.

There are hundreds of factors involved in a friendship, such as mutual interests and common experiences. However, I do know that in groups where trouble and turmoil is constant, there is little time, energy, or emotion left for either true friendship or progress. If a fighter is constantly looking over his shoulder to see what the commotion is about in his corner, he will eventually get knocked out.

Review Your Corner

This is not an easy thing to do, but we all have to review our corner from time to time. Sadly, like everything else, everyone's corner needs cleaning out and refreshing.

I have experienced this a couple of times in my life. After I got divorced and moved to Los Angeles, it was a down period in my life. I realized that some of the people I had in my corner (and in my life) were not the right people. They did not have my best interests at heart and had been in my corner for the wrong reasons. Many of them were simply self-serving.

The fact that I began reevaluating my corner during a difficult time in my life shouldn't be a surprise. Whenever we stop to take stock of our lives, it tends to be at either a very high point—when we often see that there are people around us only because they want to be on the gravy train—or during a very low point, when the untrue friends begin to jump ship. They tend to disappear during difficult times, adding to the pain we may already be experiencing. However, it is always better to find out who our true friends are.

Most of us have experienced the pain of betrayal. You confide in a friend only to find out later that the story was passed on to half a dozen other people—getting more distorted with each telling. Or a friend says one thing to your face and tells a completely different story behind your back. What's even worse is when someone you trust lies to you.

In boxing terms, it's as if a fighter's cornerman had wagered against his own fighter—not the kind of person the fighter needs in his corner. The same is true for friends. Once they have betrayed the trust you've put in them or revealed themselves as users or worse, they do not belong in your corner.

The People in Your Corner Should Be

Honest. They should be honest with you at all times. Telling someone what you *think* they want to hear is the easiest thing in the world. That's why it's the most common kind of advice—and ultimately, the most useless. A true friend is someone who will risk hurting your feelings by telling you something you may not want—but need—to hear. I want nothing less than honesty from the people around me. If I am wearing something unflattering, I want to know it. If I am about to make a wrong decision, I want someone to point it out. And if I say or do something inappropriate, I want to be told.

Helpful. You should be able to call this person at any time of the day or night if you really need him or her. Make certain that if you called this friend at midnight because you were stranded with a disabled car, he or she wouldn't mutter "Call a taxi" into the phone, and roll over to go back to sleep. A true member of your support team should be there for you 24/7 and vice versa.

Intelligent. Try to select people whose intelligence is equal or superior to your own. This doesn't necessarily mean someone who has a college degree but someone with good basic intelligence and street smarts. I try to surround myself with smart people. Some are book smart and others are street smart. In either case, I listen to their opinions and advice.

Successful. Success is often contagious. Show me a loser and I'll show you a person who is often surrounded by other losers. Birds of a feather really do flock together. Successful, productive people have little time for those who waste their time and energy. I don't measure success just in terms of money. A person who works hard and is happy in his work is a success. Look for people who smile a lot. They must be doing something right.

Trustworthy. It's important to select friends who can keep a secret. When you tell someone something extremely personal, it's important that it won't become common knowledge within hours. If you feel uncomfortable telling someone an intimate detail of your life, they do not belong in your inner circle.

Worthy of your respect. It's important to be able to respect the people with whom you spend your time. They don't have to earn more than you or have a wall full of framed academic degrees, but they should be worthy of your respect. Likewise, it is important that they respect you. With respect comes trust.

On your side. Select friends who have your best interests at heart. People who tell you that you look great when you know you don't and those who offer what you know to be the wrong advice often have a hidden agenda. Some people are great at acting like a friend, when in reality they don't really have your back. They would betray you in a second. Get rid of them.

Well liked. Look for a person who is well liked by others. If everyone you know hates this person and you get odd looks every time his or her name comes up, there must be a reason why. Pay attention. A friend of mine dated a man who everyone hates. We tried to tell her that this guy was not what she thought he was, and we pointed out all the red flags. It wasn't until he cheated on her and stole money from her that she caught on.

Unselfish. You want someone in your corner who is unselfish. Selfishness is not just a matter of money but of time and energy as well. I had a friend who would call me every single day and spend half an hour discussing her problems. I would listen to her, and at the end of the half hour I would say something like, "Guess what happened to me today?" She would respond by saying, "Well, I have to go now, bye!" Everyone goes through rough periods when he or she needs more attention than usual, but there are people who always need your attention and offer very little in return. Usually these are the type of people who float from one friend to another.

STICK TO THE FIGHT PLAN

A boxer does his homework. Weeks and months before he enters the ring, he will collect every video he can of his opponent's fights. Through watching these tapes, a boxer learns an opponent's weaknesses, strengths, and fighting styles. He will watch them, again and again—wearing out the pause and rewind buttons on his VCR in the process. He may have sat ringside and watched his opponent box a half-dozen or more times. Perhaps he's even fought him in the past. But he will still study the tapes closely. This is how he creates his strategy for the upcoming fight.

Whatever strategy he develops is based on the opponent he will face. Remember, what works in one case may not work in another. A good fighter knows not only the fighter he will be facing but the fighter's style as well. Through the tapes he can accurately assess the way the boxer fought in the past and is likely to fight in the future.

The good fighter will also review tapes of his own fights against fighters with the same style as his upcoming opponent, studying them with his whole team—as a group and separately. His manager will hire sparring partners who have a similar style as that opponent. Going into the bout, every member of the team should know the strengths and weaknesses of both his fighter and his opponent.

It is this information that helps a boxer and his team to form a strategy for both the fight and the training regime. They look for very specific things in those tapes. They search for strategies or moves that have worked well against that fighter in the past. Is he a slugger who moves in close and tries to overpower his opponents? Does he move around a lot in the ring, looking for a sure opening before punching? Is he still going strong during the later rounds of a fight, or does he tire easily? There are literally dozens of different boxing styles and just as many ways to counter each one.

By the time the boxer and his team are finished, the upcoming fight will have become a carefully choreographed battle. Weeks before the first bell, the team may have developed a strategy that maps out the entire fight, round by round. Their fight plan will include both a general strategy and specific tactics. The overall strategy may be to tire out an opponent in the first four or five rounds and then fight aggressively in the later rounds. It may also include tactics such as looking for an opening on an opponent's left side. A good fighter and his corner will leave as little as possible to chance.

As with every aspect of a fighter's preparation, the fight plan serves two roles. First and foremost, it provides him with a strategy for the fight. Second, the fight plan allows him to walk into the ring with a sense of confidence born of knowledge. He knows what to expect from his opponent and what he can do to counter the worst his opponent has to offer.

In your own life, fight plans are a bit harder to formulate. After all, in the ring, there are only a certain number of fighting styles, a certain number of moves, and a physically limited space to do battle. In life, the combinations are virtually limitless. For example, take bosses. Is your boss or immediate supervisor formal and all business or more casual and easygoing? Is he apt to lose his temper easily? Does he blame his mistakes on his underlings?

It helps to recognize what type of person you are dealing with in every situation and react accordingly. We usually do this automatically and unconsciously. Anyone who has ever faced a new boss the first day of work or can recall her most recent first date can remember what it is like. You are constantly looking for clues about the person's management style or personality. You automatically match it to your own ideas of what that person requires in terms of job performance or to your own personal style.

I try to create a fight plan for every situation. I decide how to approach a particular project or problem, and I write down my thoughts and ideas, making a list of pros and cons. It's amazing how much it helps to put it down on paper. I keep a notepad next to my bed, another one in the bathroom, and a third in my car. Whenever a thought or idea pops up, I jot it down.

In each new situation you find yourself, whether it's business or personal, be aware of where you are and pay attention to the clues that appear all around you. Your gut reaction is usually accurate. Be true to yourself. Your first reaction is usually accurate. A fighter who fights in a style unsuited to him is bound to lose. And a woman who changes her life entirely for her boyfriend or husband is destined to be unhappy. Find a way to adapt your personal style to whomever you are facing. In boxing this is called "fighting your own fight." It is simply finding a way to deal with a situation that best suits your own unique style. Doing this, however, means that you have to know the strong and weak points of your opponent as well as yourself. It means formulating a fight plan and sticking to it.

When it became apparent that my divorce was unavoidable, I decided to move on in every way. I wanted, as so many women in my position do, a fresh start. I decided that the best plan for me was to pick up, leave town, and begin anew. I hated the thought of leaving my family, but I knew it would be good for me to make a change in my life.

The first thing I did was decide on a city. I set down a list of criteria for my new city. I knew I needed a good neighborhood to live in, major media outlets, access to top-notch fighters and gyms, and friends. Those requirements narrowed my list to a handful of places. I decided on Los Angeles. I flew out to California to evaluate the situation and prepare my fight plan.

I was familiar enough with the city to be able to get around easily, as I'd recently been spending quite a bit of time there and liked it. Within a few weeks, I created a list of what I would need in my new city and set about pulling it together—an apartment, a hairdresser, a doctor, a dentist, and a new bank. I did everything methodically, and a few weeks later, I was in Los Angeles. The move was a total success, largely because of the advance research and planning I'd done prior to the decision and the move. How you arrive at your goal is often just as important as picking the right goal.

Fights can be won or lost depending on the fight plan. A good plan shifts the odds in the fighter's favor. However, a bad plan, which typically doesn't include enough preparation, is of little or no help. Another danger arises when fighters don't stick to their plan once they get into the ring. I have seen great fighters lose matches unnecessarily because they didn't stick to their fight plan. They worked hard for months before fight time. They prepared and worked out a detailed strategy and adapted their training based on that strategy. Then they climbed into the ring, followed the strategy for the first round, and suddenly started improvising. Sometimes a trainer can talk a fighter back into following the plan between rounds. Other times, the boxer is knocked out before the bell rings to signal the end of the round.

Several years ago, one of my fighters, Bronco McKart, was fighting a guy named Winky Wright. They are both gifted boxers, but I felt that Bronco knew exactly what he had to do and when to do it. When he got into the ring, inexplicably, he didn't follow the fight plan, and he lost. He ended up fighting Wright a total of three times in his career, and Wright won all three. When a fighter doesn't follow through on the fight plan, it is one of the most painful things in the sport to witness. He has prepared himself to win, probably even worked hard toward that goal. Yet he lost by second-guessing himself in the heat of battle. In these cases, the preparation and training weren't wasted, but the victory—the winning—was unnecessarily squandered.

There are many reasons why a fighter doesn't stick to the fight plan. Sometimes a fighter panics or becomes impatient waiting for results. In some cases, he is used to winning and becomes arrogant. Quite frankly, it doesn't matter why he abandoned the plan. What matters is that he lost unnecessarily. Improvisation or "winging it" should be the last resort in almost any situation and only used if the original plan isn't working. You have to stick with what you know will work.

On the other hand, there often is a point in time when you *should* turn to impromptu tactics. This, naturally, is a judgment call. However, the most common mistake is improvising too soon. The advice that I offer my fighters is that if they have a fight plan, even if it doesn't seem to be setting the world on fire, as long as it isn't failing completely, stick with it. The odds are usually with the fighters who stick to the plan.

The times in life when I have been most successful are the times I stuck to my original plan. I have plotted out a course for an event or a promotion and followed it to a T. I can look at my failures and with hindsight tell exactly where I went wrong. It was usually because I deviated from my original blueprint.

To prepare an effective fight plan or strategy, you should not only look at your opponent and his strengths or weaknesses but take a long honest look at yourself as well. This scrutiny will assist you to prepare more thoroughly. *A fight plan—or any plan—is only as good as the information you bring to it. If you are working with inferior or incomplete information, then your chances for success are hindered. Very often, the difference between a good fight plan and a poor one is simply paying attention.* For example, the fighter who watches the videotapes and sees that his opponent is what is known as an inside fighter, who moves in quickly for the kill, will automatically devise a training regime that targets the opponent's weak points.

A good fight plan acknowledges your weaknesses and works to turn them around. Anyone who tells you that he or she doesn't have any weaknesses is either very foolish or lying to themselves. At the heart of every good fight plan is a merciless honesty. When developing a fight plan, you have to be absolutely honest with yourself regarding your strong and weak points and those of your opponent. Know your limitations. Don't overestimate yourself or underestimate the other guy.

I very rarely allow myself to be fooled by others, and more

important, by myself. However, one instance sticks out in which I allowed both to happen. I remember one fighter I represented who was a great prospect. He had all the makings of a champion. I had a whole plan as to how I wanted to get him to the world championship. When we were offered one particular match, he insisted that we ask for a six-figure deal. I knew the figure he wanted was far too much to ask at this point in his career. But I was still relatively new to the business, and relatively new as a manager to this particular fighter, so I listened to him instead of my own heart. I thought that I would prove myself by landing this six-figure deal. If I could do that, then it would boost not only my fighter's career, but my own as well. Needless to say, when I asked for that purse, the promoters refused. By then I was committed to the sum, however, and we soon reached an impasse. We ended up walking away from the fight, even when they were offering a fair amount for a bout that would have helped my client's career.

Naturally, I had a fight plan going into these negotiations. I had researched and was prepared to explain why this large sum of money should be paid. I had facts and figures at my fingertips. And it worked, but only up to a point. The goal I had set was simply unreasonable. In asking for that much money for the bout, I was not only letting ego get the best of me, but I was being fundamentally dishonest with myself. It was a mistake I never made again.

Outside the ring, developing a fight plan allows you to think through your strategy in a calm and collected way, long before the fight ahead. The gathering of information and formulating a logical strategy can only increase your chances of winning when the time comes to step into the ring. The fight plan is the most important aspect of your preparation.

In a business setting, the salesman will learn as much as possible about his prospective client's operation so that he presents his products to the client's best advantage. Just as a fighter has to tailor his fight to each opponent, so must we change our approach to each challenge. What worked in one situation may not work in a different situation. For instance, when an employee goes in to ask for a raise, he might spend some time noting previous achievements. This should include added responsibilities, improvement in quality or quantity of work: anything that is verifiable. Doing this in advance, without the pressure of sitting across from the boss, allows him to make as complete a list as possible. It also allows him to formulate answers to any possible objections. However, all that work would be wasted if once he entered the office, he changed his plan. Instead of saying, "I want a raise because of A, B, and C," he said, "I need a raise because my child's tuition went up." The fact that school tuition increased may be as true and verifiable as any of the reasons that were calmly listed before the meeting, but it isn't the strongest argument.

Just as an accurate map assists you to get from one place to another in the most direct way, a well-drawn fight plan guides you through any possible situation. It should move you forward and help you navigate around objections or obstacles.

Outside the ring, our battles are more private. When you turn to someone in your corner for help with your boss, a client, or a relationship, you can't bring tapes for them to study along with you. They may know the people involved, and obviously that helps. However, in most cases the best you can do is describe what happened or what is about to happen. This is where the problems start. We're all tempted to present ourselves in the best possible light. It's only natural that we want to be seen as the good guy in any conflict. However, if you are approaching someone in your corner for advice, be warned that the quality of advice can only be as good as the information you provide. As they say in the world of computers: garbage in—garbage out.

For example, suppose you approach a friend for advice on how to talk to your boss about a promotion. You list all of your accomplishments, such as the new business you've brought to the company, the many trips you've taken on behalf of the firm, and all of your other successful efforts, large and small. All of these contributions are no doubt true. However, if you've neglected to mention to your friend that one of the company's biggest clients left and went to the competition, that you've been late for work several times in the past few weeks, and that the boss just discovered that you were having an affair at the office, the advice you receive will be worthless, if not harmful. Based on the information you provided, your friend may suggest an aggressive approach when you ask for a promotion. If your friend knew the entire story, however, her advice might be quite different. When the boss denies your request for a promotion, you can, of course, go back to your corner and assume the part of the victim. But a fight strategy is not about coming out a victim. It's about winning.

When my kids were still in school, I thought it was essential that they take a course in creative writing. I had and still have a whole list of reasons why I think writing is an important part of a child's education. I could have stood up in front of the school board, PTA, or any other group that would listen to me, and given my reasons. They might have even agreed to take it under advisement. A committee might have been formed to study the issue, and perhaps a report would have been written. But my sons probably would have been in their second year of college before I heard from them. Rather than go that route, I formed a plan in which I stated my reasons for the program, then offered a proposal in which I volunteered to teach the class. The creative-writing program was a reality in a matter of weeks.

As calculating as it may seem, the same is true for relationships. They require game plans, too. If you have a conflict with a friend, lover, or spouse, take a few minutes to formulate a plan of action. Make a list of your complaints and, even more important, a list of what you hope to accomplish by confronting that person. Not only will this allow you to organize your thoughts, but it will give you time to cool down and calmly study the situation. In my experience, very rarely is anything accomplished when two people just come out swinging wildly at one another. In fact, very often someone swings below the belt in the heat of battle, saying things that would have never been said if he or she had sat down and formulated a fight plan.

Looking back on my marriage, I can now see that there were many times when I should have planned things out better. I sometimes acted on impulse instead of thinking a situation out. It was a lesson well learned, though, and I now take the time to strategize more.

A Fight Plan Checklist

Here is a multistep program for developing a professional fight plan. Follow these steps and you will be able to define your goal, identify obstacles that may stand in your way, work on your weak points, and build on your assets. It is essential that you are absolutely honest with yourself when answering these questions. After all, the worst mistake anyone can make is fooling himself that the competition is weaker—or he is stronger—than is the case.

☐ Do you have a clearly defined long-term goal?

☐ Formulate a plan to achieve your goal based on your understanding of how others have achieved the same goal. Divide it into short-term goals.

☐ What skills do you have that make you uniquely qualified to reach your long-term goal?

☐ How can you use those skills in your current situation to achieve your short-term goals?

☐ What skills can you acquire that can help you reach your goal more quickly?

❑ What sources of information are the most valuable for preparing to reach your goal?

❑ List at least five things that could possibly hold you back.

❑ For each of the five obstacles you've listed, list three things you can do to eliminate them.

Winning rarely, if ever, happens by accident. The championship career is the product of a long string of victories and well-fought fights. The perfect fight comes from a long string of days spent in the gym. And the perfect day in the gym comes from a well-planned training regime.

In our own lives the situation is very similar. There is no such thing as accidental success. A country-western singer once said, "They call me an overnight success. Well, it sure was one hell of a long night."

To Do List

Nobody has a successful career by accident. Large successes are built on a string of small victories that take place over years, months, weeks, right on down to days. If you take even a little time to consider this, you can see how each day is vitally important. That's why I've always kept my own, personal, daily "to do" list. Life today is incredibly hectic and fast paced. Whether you are a professional, a homemaker, a part-time worker, or self-employed, you probably feel the pressure to accomplish more in a shorter amount of time than ever before. By making daily "to do" lists, you will organize your day in the most efficient way and will work more efficiently as well.

Another benefit of the "to do" list is that it offers you the ability to really take a long, hard look at your life on a daily basis. At the end of the week, or even each day, you can look back and either see just how much you accomplished or plan more efficiently to get more done. The following typifies the perfect daily "to do" list that I've used for years:

<u>Calls to Be Made Today</u>

The person's name.

Phone number (why waste time looking it up?).

Reason for the call.

Best time of day to call.

Topics that should be mentioned during the call.

<u>Errands</u>

Where you are going.

Purpose for errand. Be specific.

Name of person you have to see or meet.

<u>Work-Related Items</u>

Projects due.

Projects to be started.

Necessary research or planning needed for current projects.

Just Go for It . . . Maybe

It is very easy to say "Follow your dream and risk it all." However, that is often neither possible nor desirable. I know a young man who spent ten years in the insurance business. One day he walked into his supervisor's office and just quit. He wanted to dedicate his life to his first love—music. Well, if you can imagine the look his boss gave him, try to imagine his wife's reaction. Yes, it was impulsive and romantic, perhaps even the kind of story you'd see in a movie or hear about a rock star. But this was a disaster. His music career stalled in small clubs, and he ran through his life savings in a matter of months. He became more and more frustrated with not becoming an instant star. He was ultimately forced to take a much-lower-paying job in—what else—insurance. The entire experience left him bitter and defeated.

There were many things he could have done, such as planning the move into music to take place more slowly, and playing weekends or during his vacations. He could have done more research into the music business. And he certainly could have prepared financially for the life change. He took a huge gamble without planning or adequately preparing. He never looked at what he was risking, only at the possible rewards.

For most of us, the decisions we make are not as extreme, yet they can impact our lives just as much. My stepfather, for example, had a wonderful career at a Detroit car company. There he enjoyed personal satisfaction, good pay, and a pleasant working environment. Then he found his dream house, on eighty acres of lovely property. The only problem was that the house was more than fifty miles from his office. He faced a hard choice: He could give up the job he loved and risk finding a new job closer to the house, or he could give up the once-in-a-lifetime opportunity to buy such a house. He studied the problem and eventually made the decision to commute three hours a day. In the best of all possible worlds, my stepfather's dream house would have been down the block from his office. It wasn't, yet he found a way to make it all work.

Unfortunately, none of us live in the best of all possible worlds. In fact, we live in an imperfect world. Priorities are what help us navigate through the imperfections. When we make decisions based on priorities we set for ourselves, we know what we are sacrificing and what we are gaining. There's no shame in making these compromises. They're what allow us to move forward in our careers and our personal lives.

Almost as important as picking the fight is selecting the

location. I'm always fascinated when I see a couple arguing in public. Almost always, it's over something trivial, and almost always, both of them are at a disadvantage. Whoever wins the fight probably doesn't gain much; in fact, he or she stands to lose more in the way of hard feelings and embarrassment. Neither party is at his or her best, so he or she can't get their points across effectively. Yet either one or both of them made the decision to fight at that particular time. These fights turn out to be pointless—and usually worse than pointless—because both of their days were probably ruined by the conflict. The winner, I would wager, doesn't go away feeling very much like a winner.

You can go crazy fighting every battle that comes your way. The world throws a million jabs at us every day in the way of slights, annoyances, and petty conflicts. You have to decide which ones are worth your time and effort. You should weigh every situation and decide if it's worth fighting over. Is it worth getting upset over? My answer is almost always "no." Your time and energy are too valuable to waste on small fights. Is it worth it to fight over a parking space? A place in line?

Some fighters are "boxers." That means they use a lot of fancy footwork and moves to bob and weave around their opponents' punches while they wait for an opening. They are called outside fighters because they maintain a distance from their opponents, working their punches in from the outside.

The other type of fighter is the banger or puncher. They stand relatively still and punch their opponents. They are called inside fighters because they like to get in close, where their punches can be most effective.

One of the most important factors of a fight is negotiated long before the first tickets are sold: the size of the ring. The outside fighter almost always favors a large ring, ranging anywhere from twenty to twenty-four feet across. The size provides an abundance of space in which to move around and implement his individual style. The larger ring gives him the chance to use his footwork and move to his full advantage against his opponent. The inside fighter will always favor the smaller sixteen- to eighteen-foot ring. He can use the smaller space to back his opponent into the corners, or against the ropes, and quickly win the bout. These styles come naturally to fighters. Each can be equally effective in its own way, given the proper training and dedication.

Just as fighters have their ideal ring size, we each have our ideal environments for our jobs and relationships. A large corporation that allows employees to move quickly up the ladder from one department to another is the environment best suited to "corporate outside boxers." A smaller firm, however, allows the "corporate inside fighter" to focus in on a narrow area of expertise for several years. He may not have much upward mobility through different departments, but he can stand out in his one area. As with fighters, there is no right or wrong style. Each can be equally effective given the suitable environment, training, and preparation.

In relationships, we can apply the inside and outside principles to the type of attention a person requires. This is not to imply in any way that he or she is locked in constant battle. It simply means that people need their own amount of space to carry on a successful relationship. Some require a small emotional ring in which they have nearly constant closeness to their lover, spouse, or friends. They require frequent contact with those they care about and who care about them. Others need more emotional room within a relationship and the ability to move about freely.

Following are lists of the characteristics of inside and outside fighters. Again, no one style is right or wrong. It entirely depends on the individual. At different points in your life, you may change styles. You may even have different styles for work and play. However, it does pay to identify those inside and outside traits in yourself when considering a new romance or job.

Inside Fighter

Enjoys close personal relationships at work and thrives as part of a team.

Needs only one special person in her life.

Is happier with a small, tightly knit group of friends.

Doesn't like to travel or relocate frequently.

Enjoys the domestic pleasures of cooking, caring for children, and watching a movie at home with family.

Outside Fighter

Craves the high-pressure and adrenaline-fueled rush of a fast-moving office where he has to think on his feet.

Doesn't want to be tied down to just one person.

Enjoys meeting new people—the more the merrier.

A new city and a new job are the ultimate adventure.

Enjoys going out to a new restaurant or bar.

Remember, there are no iron-clad rules. Most of us are combinations of inside and outside fighters. Just as it is important to take an honest look at yourself and identify your own style, it is also important not to limit yourself to one particular style or type of opponent. That kind of thinking is simply self-defeating.

If you really want to take on a challenge, then identify the weak points in your style and work on them. You can do this either by adapting your own style to meet the new challenge or by learning an entirely new set of skills that better prepare you to take on the task. In the ring, this is a process of maturation, through which a fighter tests and stretches his talents. It is not that much different outside the ring, where we should all be willing to grow in our careers and our personal lives.

LET'S GET READY TO RUMBLE

Losers have a million different excuses and stories to explain how they lost. Sometimes they accept responsibility for their defeat, but most often they blame someone or something else. Interestingly, a lot of them are already thinking about losing before they even step into the ring. After all, it takes time to think of a good story or excuse. It takes time to become comfortable with it, so that losing doesn't seem like such a tragedy. Those are the times when losing is almost a self-fulfilled prophesy.

In contrast, all winners think alike. Even before a fight, there is no doubt in the winner's mind that he will win it. He's chosen the fight carefully. He's planned, prepared, and trained for the moment when he steps into the ring. He knows exactly what he has to do and when he should do it. If he loses, it's a genuine surprise. Winning is a matter of self-confidence and good self-esteem.

Self-doubt, second thoughts, and fear have no place in a winner's thinking. After all he's sacrificed and labored, he knows in his heart that not only should he win, but that he deserves to win. Truthfully, he might not win. Nobody wins every fight he takes on. But during that walk from the locker room to the ring, every good fighter has set his mind on the victory ahead. Just as he's prepared his body and fighting technique, he's also prepared his thinking for the job in the ring and the victory ahead. Some of this is long-term mental preparation. Surprisingly, much of this confidence naturally comes with physical preparation and training.

Boy, does this translate directly to everyday life. Having a positive, winning attitude makes all the difference in the world. In the media world today, they call it "spinning." A smart person can take any situation and spin it into something positive. Over the years, I have learned to master this technique. I consider it to be one of my finest tools.

The better prepared you are to meet a challenge, the less intimidating that challenge becomes and the more confidence you have in your abilities. This has to do with the entire process of identifying the challenge, formulating a solution, and preparing yourself to act on that solution. This holds true whether it's a job, a relationship, or a hobby. After you've worked on your fighting maneuvers and strategy, your confidence is the last thing that needs adjusting. For a fighter, the minutes of final preparation are absolutely crucial to the fight that follows. It is then that he summons all of his willpower and passion. It's that strength and confidence which propels the winner out of the locker room, into the ring, and very often to victory.

The good fighter knows in his mind that the fight is winnable. The people in his corner can encourage him, but the fighter has to absolutely believe in his ultimate victory himself. When Muhammad Ali (then Cassius Clay) stepped up at a young age to fight the boxing legend Sonny Liston, only a tiny number of sportswriters and experts gave Ali a chance to triumph over the world champion. Perhaps they didn't like the young fighter's brash style or constant stream of jokes and poems. But Ali, despite his youth, was confident in his abilities in the ring. When he stepped into the ring in 1964, he did so with an impressive string of victories behind him and total self-confidence.

A fighter who allows doubt, fear, or any other form of negative thinking to overwhelm him is working *for* his opponent. The more he doubts, the more work he's doing for his opponent. Think about it. A fighter wouldn't do a single push-up if he thought it would benefit the competition, and a business executive wouldn't write a single line of a report for a competing company. Self-doubt can do more to serve the competition than a thousand push-ups or a hundred reports.

Hundreds of people have written on the power of positive thinking. Some of the claims have been far-fetched, others more modest, but to be a winner, you have to think like a winner when entering any arena. Thinking like a winner means walking into a situation with absolute confidence and with absolute focus on the job at hand. This confidence is largely a by-product of smart physical and strategic preparation. The focus, on the other hand, comes through thorough *mental* preparation.

Fighters make their last-minute mental preparations for the big fight differently. I've known fighters who send their trainers and the rest of their corner out of the locker room several minutes before a fight so they can lie down, review strategy, meditate, and give every bit of concentration to the fight ahead. These fighters might visualize their opponents losing. Imagining the fight in their mind's eye, they picture how they will land the knockout punch that sends their opponent to the mat. They can see themselves bobbing and weaving around their opponent's punches. Their minds are completely focused on the job ahead.

Other fighters require outside stimulus. They'll have the locker room packed with friends and their team and loud music blasting from a boom box. Everyone will shout encouragement or pound on the steel lockers. All of the energy and good feelings in the room flow toward the fighter. By the time these guys slip on their robes and head into the arena, their adrenaline is already pumping.

You may have experienced something like this when driving or walking to work while listening to a song on the radio or a Walkman. The song pumps you up so that you begin the day with a bang. The same thing holds true for these fighters. The music, the yelling, and the encouragement increase their energy levels, while the people around them drive out all hint of doubt as to the outcome of the fight.

From my years of experience, I've learned that there is no right or wrong way to prepare. What works for one person might not work for another. The challenge is to find out what works best for you and what works best for the people around you when your job is to be in *their* corner. Eliminate all negative elements, thoughts, and self-doubt. Any negative thinking can only hurt you at this stage.

In the ring, a split second of doubt can lead to disaster. All it takes is a moment of hesitation for the opponent to land a knock-out punch. Outside the ring, a person's anxiety, doubt, and most of all, fear can show up just as clearly. You may have prepared harder than the competition, but if you enter a situation giving off an aura of self-doubt, the other person or persons will sense it and react accordingly. Act confident. Believe you are right. Prove your point. But do it with class and compassion.

When faced with an opponent, how can you expect his respect if you don't respect yourself? A salesman can be selling the best product in his field, yet if he goes to pitch a customer and hesitates or stumbles—if he lacks confidence—then the customer will instinctively begin doubting the product. Those doubts are communicated in a person's speech, body language, and most of all, performance. They can negate the results of all the hard work, sacrifice, and preparation. They can turn a winner into a loser.

I'm a firm believer that we should pump ourselves up every day. Look in the mirror and tell yourself that you look great. Don't fixate on a blemish, bad hair, or a few extra pounds. Most people won't notice it, anyhow. Just stand tall and go enjoy your day.

It doesn't matter if you're going to a high-powered job in a large office or staying home to take care of the kids. When you focus entirely on the job at hand, you feel better and perform better. Whether you need loud music and high energy to fire you up, or tranquility and meditation, get the job done.

I know this is difficult. Most of us wake up and go to the same job every day. As in the movie *Groundhog Day*, some of our lives are very repetitious. We need to raise our energy levels nevertheless. It could be something as simple as listening to a song you like or getting or giving a kind word of encouragement from or to your spouse. Whether we turn inward or outward to increase our confidence and energy level, the results are dramatic and noticeable to the people around us as well as to ourselves.

One of the best parts of my life is my speaking career. I love speaking to college groups, women's symposiums, health seminars, and female empowerment groups. No matter how many times

I do it, I still look forward to each one. I begin my preparation for these presentations by allowing myself enough time to master the material at hand, then slowly formulate my presentation. As the date of the engagement approaches, I think about what I hope to accomplish. I select what I'm going to wear and pack for the trip. By the time I get there, I feel confident, excited about meeting so many new people, and enthusiastic about my message.

The feeling of confidence is like a vitamin. It energizes me. I try to make it seem as though I am speaking to a room full of friends. I know my material, seldom use notes, and speak from my heart. I believe that's what makes it work for me. I have seen other people stumble or stall on key points while giving a presentation simply because they weren't properly prepared or did not have confidence in themselves.

Fake It until You Make It

The expression "fake it until you make it" can be interpreted many different ways. A cynical interpretation is that some people, essentially braggarts, think they can succeed by talking and acting the part of a true champion, but they don't present a convincing picture. The interpretation I prefer is that the top fighters project a champion's confidence and attitude even before stepping into the ring. This doesn't mean bragging, but exuding a quiet confidence. The best fighters walk and talk with confidence, and they consider themselves champions from the time they start training for their first bout. They eat right, train right, and think like champs.

Many successful entrepreneurs acted successful before they actually were. They drove the right car, joined the right clubs, and frequented the right restaurants. They networked with people who could further their careers, and they gave the impression that they were on equal ground with them. It worked.

There are also patterns and habits that identify winners and losers. The difference, of course, is that a winner's attitude and habits take hard work, whereas a loser's habits are easy to fall into.

To look at winners—in the gym, on the street, or in a social set-ting—you would think that they've been champs for years, when, in fact, they don't have the record to back up the attitude. What they do have is the confidence that they possess the ability and potential to be champs. They are just waiting for the opportunity to make it a reality.

The first thing anyone you meet learns about you is how you feel about yourself. Whatever signals you give will be taken with more than a grain of salt. After all, who better to know your own self-worth than you? The employee who belittles his own job or company isn't presenting a very flattering picture of himself. If the company is a horrible place to work, then what's he doing there? Can't he find something better? If his job is unimportant and boring, what does that say about him? That his superiors don't trust him with the interesting and important assignments?

True champions take pride in their abilities and skills. Natu-rally these fighters have doubts. Perhaps they are even a little afraid. But they turn those doubts and fears around by training harder and longer than any other fighter in the gym. If they doubt their ability to hit hard, then they'll train to punch harder. Little by little, they will train away any doubts they may have secretly har-bored. And most of all, they won't display those doubts for the world to see. They may ask their trainers or certain people in their corner to help with certain aspects of their fight, but they won't advertise their weaknesses to the general public. They never wear their insecurities on their sleeves. Once fighters start viewing them-selves as champions, it doesn't take long before others start view-ing them in the same light. These are the fighters who get a chance to prove their talents with promoters and the audience. What these fighters do is prepare for winning, even when they are just start-ing out or are dispirited.

Understandably, this isn't easy. There are times in all of our lives when we don't feel like champs. Perhaps we've just suffered a setback in our careers or in a relationship. Our "mental game" isn't what it used to be or should be. Inside we might be feeling like we've been knocked out in the first round of every fight we've ever entered into. But that is exactly the time to really start boosting our confidence. It's easy to feel like a champ when we're winning all the time, but a lot harder to muster the championship spirit after a defeat. Still, we need to project a strong front. We should see ourselves as champs, feel it, taste it. Imagine what it feels like. I'm a strong believer in visualization. Just as a basketball player might foresee the ball going into the net before he makes the shot, I try to imagine myself coming out on top in any situation before entering into it. If I'm nervous or scared, I never let anyone see that.

Champ Checklist

These principles apply to champions in all walks of life.

Champs always train hard and train smart. They prepare themselves to win both physically and mentally. The effort they put out is in direct proportion to how badly they want to win. Show me fighters who are lazy in their fight preparation, and I'll show you fighters planning to lose. In business, when a business owner is about to merge with another company, he will put in weeks (maybe months) of preparation and research. He will strategize precisely.

Champs always treat themselves and their bodies as valuable assets. Amazingly, people abuse their own bodies with drugs, cigarettes, alcohol, and lack of exercise. Yet many of these same people keep their cars in perfect condition. They feel that the slightest nick or scratch on the body is a major catastrophe, even as they fill their own bodies with poisons. True champs know their bodies and minds are like a Rolls Royce and treat them accordingly. Good health is essential to success. It's hard to run a household or a business when you are flat on your back in the hospital. Eat as healthy as possible and get enough rest. Don't burn out.

Champs always demand and deserve respect. For many bullies, it's a constant battle to demand respect from others. Whether out on the street or in corporate headquarters, a bully is a bully. They threaten and intimidate others to get what they call respect. They use these tactics because they have done nothing to deserve or earn that respect. The people they intimidate are simply buckling under to avoid some unpleasantness. True champs not only deserve the respect of others but receive it freely, without having to resort to bullying tactics. When you show that you respect yourself and others, it encourages people to give that respect back to you.

Champs always share the credit with others. Nobody makes it on his or her own. Everyone has had others contribute to his or her success, even champions. The real champs acknowledge this fact and feel a sense of pride in sharing the credit. In the end, it is only pride that makes people steal the limelight or take credit for someone else's idea or work. Give credit where it is due.

Champs always respect their opponents. Champs want a fight worthy of their talents and skills. If they've chosen their fights carefully, then they must assume that anyone who steps into the ring is a worthy opponent, making their victories all the more rewarding. Never run anyone else down just to make yourself seem better. It always backfires. The fighter who calls his opponent a bum before the fight ends up looking foolish if he happens to get beat by this "bum."

Champs always respect the sport. What does it say about you if you're involved in a career or a relationship that you don't respect and badmouth it to others? I have met champions who don't care for their opponents, but it's a rare champ who doesn't love the sport to which he dedicates so much time and energy. Whatever career you have chosen, whatever life partner you have selected, or whatever decision you make—respect it.

You should act like a champ before you reach that goal because how you *act* can have a great impact on how you *think*. The best fighters have bad days. They may feel tired, depressed, or generally unmotivated. Yet somehow, when they hit the gym, they will give their all to their training, no matter how bad they may feel. They will continue to train like champs, no matter how much they may just want to stay in bed with the covers pulled up over their heads. And then something very interesting happens. After a couple of hours of hard work, they actually start to feel better, and whatever it was that bothered them just a short while ago no longer seems all that important.

As silly as it may sound, this happens to me when I have to clean my home. I don't start out enjoying it, but after I get going, I get into it and it actually becomes relaxing. I put on some music and the time flies by.

People are naturally drawn to winners. They feel as if that winning aura can somehow rub off on them. Winners are supported and nurtured by those in the same field. Everyone, it seems, wants to be on the same side as a winner. And what's more, people are more likely to offer winners the opportunity to prove themselves. An example of this in a business setting is a boss that has two salespeople who both bring in exactly the same amount of business. Yet when the opportunity to land a big account arises, he is more likely to give the chance to the salesperson who projects a championship attitude.

Strategies for Success

Dress Like a Winner

Always dress well and with care. This doesn't mean you should go out and spend hundreds of dollars on a new Armani suit and Coach bags and shoes. Dress as well as your budget permits. Take pride in your appearance. Dress your body and groom yourself with the same care and enthusiasm as a supermodel does. Your outward appearance tells others how you feel about yourself. Whether you're a size six or a size sixteen, if you take pride in your appearance, coworkers, friends, and virtual strangers will take this as a sign of confidence and self-worth.

I can imagine many readers thinking that this is a superficial suggestion. It is true that the real worth of a person is what's inside. When you first meet someone, you usually look for clues about that person in his or her outward appearance. We all do it. It's only normal. We make snap judgments.

Dressing like a winner is easy advice to follow when things are going well in our lives, but during tough emotional times, it's just as easy to forget. When we're depressed or even just feeling a little down, it's easy to let ourselves go and shrug if off, saying, "What difference does it make, anyway?" For women especially, clothes often reflect inner feelings to the outside world. But when you're feeling the most depressed is the time you should dress like a winner. Dress depressed and people will treat you like you *are* depressed, which will only make you feel worse. Whenever you're feeling shrouded by dark moods, break out the bright colors. You'll be surprised how the upbeat colors will work to change your feelings. Spend a little extra time on your hair and makeup too. It's worth it. Before you walk out the door, add a bright accessory— a bright scarf, a pin, or another piece of jewelry.

Act Like a Winner

People love winners and shy away from losers. People want to associate professionally and personally with winners. In business and in relationships, winning breeds winning. Winners also receive the benefit of the doubt, the second chance, and the help, even when it's not needed.

There's an old saying: "Money goes to money." Wealthy women often end up with rich men. There is a common link.

Successful men end up playing golf together and belonging to the same country clubs. Just as misery loves company, so does success.

This can be difficult advice to follow when you feel like you've just lost the title match. However, keep in mind that today's loser can be tomorrow's winner. So act like it. You may have just lost the biggest battle of your professional career or personal life, yet nobody outside those in your corner need know it. If you've chosen your friends carefully, they'll not only stick with you through the good and bad times but help you get back into the ring with better training and a better fight plan. Even if you recently lost a job, got divorced, or got passed over for a promotion, tell yourself that it happened for a reason and that things will work out better for you down the line. It is often said that when one door shuts another opens.

Perform Like a Winner

A quality performance is always your best assurance for success in a relationship or on the job. Dressing like a winner and acting like a winner set the stage for you to prove yourself. It is crucial to follow through. You may look like a million bucks, hang out in all the right circles, and talk the talk. But you also have to walk the walk. When it is your turn to shine, you'd better come through. Others expect it, but more importantly, you should expect it from yourself.

Again, there are times in your life when you just don't feel like a winner. Those are the times that you can score by redoubling your effort. Perhaps even more than the success stories of winners, everybody loves a comeback story. Even if you're just coming out of a bad relationship or a problem at work, you should force yourself to get back into the ring and fight harder. It may seem like you're doing four times the amount of work for only two times the results, but that will improve. Get back up on your feet and keep fighting.

Count on the People in Your Corner

As hard as it is to admit, not everyone you know or work with is a caring person who has your best interests at heart. Despite what they say, theirs may be a momentary bond of friendship that fades quickly, or a cover for hostility. I'm amazed when friends of mine are shocked or dismayed that a coworker or casual friend broke a confidence or lied outright. My answer is always, "Why should they keep your secret or take the time to offer well-considered advice?" Not only are the consequences for them minimal, but they have no emotional investment in your well-being. By going to people like these for advice or nurturing, you leave yourself open to all kinds of low blows.

I would rather have three really good friends than a dozen half-friends. Over the years I have tried to recognize the opportunists and users who have entered my life. It's not always easy, and I have to admit that I made some mistakes along the way. I allowed myself to trust some of the wrong people, assuming that they had sincere intentions when in fact they did not.

At this stage of my life, although I have many friends and an extensive social circle, I have only a select group of people that I trust unconditionally. These are the people I turn to for advice, lean on during a crisis, and know will be there for me any time and any place. They have stood the test of time and have proven themselves to be real friends.

The Best Defense Is a Terrific Offense

People are not only drawn to winners, they are less likely to betray them. Those who spread rumors, backstab, and cheat are generally cowards or incompetent. Winners intimidate them. However, when they sense weakness or an easy target, they are likely to strike. This is how failure can breed failure. Even when you're at your lowest point, don't give these snakes an opportunity to make your situation worse. Maintain that winning attitude.

When you sense that someone has a hidden agenda, call them on it. Don't just wait for the other shoe to drop. Head it off and confront the issue. I have learned to ask, "What exactly are you trying to say?" or "Something doesn't feel right about this."

Choose All of Your Fights Carefully

Good fighters like to fight; it's what they do. Just as a good baseball player likes to play ball or a good programmer likes to problem-solve and create at the keyboard, a fighter likes to practice the skills he's worked hard to develop. The fighter, the ballplayer, and the programmer all find a measure of self-worth and accomplishment in their work. This is basic human nature. We are all drawn to what we're good at doing. And the more we do it, the better we become.

Herein lies both a blessing and a problem. Some fighters will accept almost any bout offered, if left to their own devices. They feel good about their skills and about their ability in the ring. They've put in their time at the gym, training and conditioning their bodies and minds. They feel ready to fight. They want to fight. They want to start moving up the ladder. And indeed, a lot of the times they are ready, both physically and mentally. The problem is that there is no one suitable for them to fight. Of course, there are always fighters ready to step into the ring at a moment's notice for very little money. But why waste time and effort, or worse, risk injury on a fight that means nothing?

Boxing is a sport, but it's also a career and a business. As a manager, a good deal of my time is spent planning the career paths of my fighters. An athlete's professional life is very short when compared to that of the average lawyer or accountant. He has just a few brief years to move up in the standings and earn a chance for the title.

Another common mistake new fighters make is taking on someone whom they have no hope of beating. Smart, seasoned fighters will seek out less-experienced newcomers to boost their win records. A win for the newcomer would no doubt be a major coup, but in fact he has little chance of winning. In a few years, with training and the experience that comes with additional battles, he might have an excellent chance of winning, but not at the present time. The risks of losing far outweigh the prospect of winning.

Too many people are ready to fight in everyday life. That's why there are shootings in the workplace, road rage, and other forms of unreasonable violence. Instead of conserving energy for the important battles in life, some people rant and rage about everything. They berate waiters, salespeople, and employees. They raise their voices constantly and will always take the opposite side of an argument. If someone cuts them off in traffic, they will risk life and limb to get even.

Three Reasons to Accept a Fight Engagement

Money. The fight will pay a huge amount of money, which the fighter would be absolutely foolish to turn down. Fighters, like everyone else, have rent or mortgages, car payments, and groceries to buy. A large payday allows the fighter to keep training without financial distractions and perhaps even provides investments for the future when his career is over. It's easy to see how this also applies to life outside the ring, where a person might get a job offer with a salary so large that he or she would always regret turning down the opportunity.

For some people money is a motivational factor. These people may chose a profession they don't especially enjoy solely for the financial benefits. Other people are motivated more by pleasure than money, so they will seek out a career they really love, regardless of the pay. There is no right or wrong. It is a question of what's right for you.

Exposure. It's essential to show a fighter's talents to the best possible advantage. In this way he becomes known among fans and reporters. So, too, sometimes even a lateral move at work can put you in the spotlight and show off your talents to those who matter. Remember: the right kind of positive exposure can position you and your career for worthwhile opportunities.

In my career, I have chosen certain projects because I knew the exposure would be good. The money wasn't especially great, but it led to bigger and better things. So in essence it was a wise decision.

Career move. In real life this could be the job you take in which you feel "over your head" or barely qualified to handle. Time and again I have seen fighters as well as business executives rise to meet these kinds of challenges. In boxing it is said that the title makes the man. In other words, a fighter who was not championship caliber before the title fight often becomes a champion in every way the minute he wins the title.

Depending on where a boxer is in his career, each of these reasons can have equal or varying degrees of importance. Every fight he takes on should be justified by at least one of these reasons. But it's even better if the fight is justified by two out of the three or, best yet, all three. As a negative example, I know a fighter who will fight anywhere, any time. If a promoter calls him in the morning, he will be on the plane that evening to fight in a bout that will barely cover his expenses and against an unknown opponent. He's a good fighter, with loads of heart, good technical ability, and respectable training habits. Yet his attitude toward the sport is all wrong. First, he will probably not succeed because he isn't picking his fights carefully. By filling in at the last minute for a boxer who dropped out of the match and fighting on the spur of the moment, he doesn't leave himself enough time to properly train for the bout, whereas his opponent may have been training heavily for weeks. That's assuming his opponent is of near-equal ability and standing. Second, this fighter hasn't had enough time to assemble an adequate corner. Without sufficient money or time, it's nearly impossible to put together a corner team who can offer the proper first aid, advice, or any other necessities. Third, he'll often fight in a distant city, where his opponent has the homecourt advantage. Not only will the crowd favor his opponent, but so will the local press and possibly the judges as well.

Given all of these factors, even if this boxer wins, what he has won does very little to advance his career. Beating an unknown fighter will boost his win-loss record marginally but does little for his reputation. In many cases, the opponent has nothing to lose by climbing into the ring. If the opponent loses, then he lost to a superior fighter with a higher rating. If he wins, then he's made a valuable career move. The result is that each time he agrees to one of these fights, he has more to lose than he has to gain. Whatever effort he puts into these matches is nearly always wasted.

The same rules apply to all of us in our careers and personal lives. Professional fighters have a short time in which to accomplish a lot and can't afford to take many detours along the way. We all have a finite amount of time for our careers and our personal lives. Time, whether you're a boxer or a teacher, is your most valuable commodity. Participating in fights that mean little or nothing even if you win is one of the biggest time wasters inside and outside the ring. Too often we waste time on situations, problems, and relationships that don't pay off. It's simply not worth the energy.

Think of people you know who have chosen their mates for the wrong reasons. Sometimes they marry for money, for example, then realize that they can barely stand the person.

We all know people who waste time on needless battles. They will argue with a bartender over the mixture of their whiskey sour, they'll berate employees or coworkers over a small mistake, or they'll pick arguments with their spouses over trivialities. No doubt, these are all *winnable* battles. The bartender will simply mix another drink, the coworker will redo the botched assignment, and the spouse will concede. But what is really won? Each time they engage in these pointless conflicts, they run the risk of driving people away from them. These are the people who believe you have to win at all costs. I totally disagree.

In most instances I will simply back off to avoid a confrontation. Unless the issue is of major importance to me, I won't risk a friendship just to prove that I am right. In the end, is it really important who was right and who was wrong?

A smart fighter, with smart management, will pick the proper opponent at the proper time. The fight might come at the beginning of a boxer's career, when he needs both a string of wins and media attention; during the middle of his career and the height of his powers, when he needs a strategy that positions him for the championship; or after he becomes champ, when he wants to assure his place in boxing history and amass a comfortable retirement. Similarly, we should all think ahead about which battles are worth taking on and which ones should just be conceded.

What Are You Fighting For?

I wonder why many of us waste our time and energy on unnecessary fights that result in little or no gain. Before entering into any confrontation, we should ask ourselves, "What is it we hope to gain? What is the payoff?" Here is a by-no-means-complete list of things I have found worth the time and effort of fighting for. Following this list is another one, which are things *not* worthy of anyone's time and effort. Your list may be different than mine. Think about it and make a mental list.

Worth Fighting For

1. *A principle about which you feel strongly.* It's a competitive world, and too many people are willing to cut corners to "make it." They usually end up losing. Don't let anyone talk you into some-

thing that you know in your heart is wrong. Whether it's politics, religion, or issues like abortion and the death penalty, stand strong in your convictions. At the same time, listen to and respect others' viewpoints.

2. *Protecting someone you love from harm.* Most people will fight back furiously if someone attacks their loved ones. There are few things more fierce, for example, than a mother protecting her young.

3. *A job you really want.* Fight as hard as you can to get that job. If you lose out to someone else, at least you know that you gave it your best effort. This has always been my motto. When I want something, I will fight to the very end to attain it.

4. *A better grade in school or a raise at work.* If you think you deserve better than what you received, then fight for it. However, before going into battle, have your fight plan ready. Be prepared. If you present your case intelligently, you have a good chance to get the result you were seeking.

Not Worth Fighting For

1. *Food that is served too cold, too hot, too rare, or too well done.* Ask the waiter politely to correct your order, but don't become irate. It's not his or her fault. If the service is below par, then express your dissatisfaction in the size of the tip or by not patronizing the restaurant again. People who berate servers always end up looking like total jerks.

2. *Drivers who cut you off, tailgate, steal parking spots, and so forth.* What is the point of yelling or cursing? These people are a minor annoyance at best and not worth your energy. Road rage is a total waste of time. I never give anyone the "finger." I

just smile and wave, which usually makes them feel stupid or guilty.

3. *Rude sales clerks who either ignore you or act like you don't belong in the store.* Don't let them rile you. On the other hand, don't let them intimidate you into leaving when the store has something you really want or into buying something you really don't need. Simply ignore them and find a clerk with a better attitude. Most of the salespeople in better stores work on commission, so if a clerk is rude, ask for someone else to ring up your purchase.

4. *Getting bumped from a flight or lost reservations.* Nine times out of ten it isn't the mistake of the person who tells you that your reservation was lost. Take the attitude that you both have a problem and try working it out together. In many instances, they will be the ones to call their supervisors to help put things right. I try to be the sweetest one around when there is a snafu. I immediately go into "relax" mode, take a deep breath, and figure out the best way to handle the situation.

Pick battles that you truly believe you can win. A recent college graduate, for instance, if given control over a Fortune 500 company would stand as much chance of success as a Golden Gloves fighter against the World Heavyweight Champion. With a few years of training and experience, both could very well develop their potential and succeed if they choose the fights in between carefully. Try not to bite off more than you can chew. In other words, be careful what you wish for . . . you may get it.

Remember, choosing your fights doesn't mean making choices based solely on your ability to win. I know fighters who will only fight opponents they *know* they can beat rather than take on someone who is more of a challenge. These fighters have 20–0 records, but all of their matches are against unknown fighters. Boxers are rated by the number of fights they've had, the quality of their opposition, and the percentage of wins versus losses. A fighter who settles for the easy wins may have a high win-loss ratio but not the respect of his peers or the fans. They've taken the safe way. They may retire from the sport with a perfect record, but they've never tested their potential, and once they retire, they'll never know how good they might have been. These are the fighters who settle. Apply that to your own experiences. The less one risks, the less there is to be gained.

Money, career advancement, and media exposure are the factors that boxing managers consider when picking fights. Obviously, these same criteria can't be applied to every job, much less relationships. However, what they do is remind us to ask two basic questions before we enter into any argument or situation. Those questions are: "What do I have to gain by this?" and "What do I have at stake?" This is the most basic business principle of risk versus reward, yet it's amazing how many people forget to apply it. For instance, you wouldn't commute a long distance to a low-paying job that offered little in the way of job satisfaction. However, if that job advanced your career or offered you recognition within your chosen field, the commute would be well worth the inconvenience.

Stress for Success

A little bit of stress can be a good thing. It gets the adrenaline pumping, motivates you, and helps to focus your attention on the job at hand. When you're about to do something difficult, whether it's stepping into the ring for a heavyweight championship bout or stepping into a high-powered office, this is good. However, too much stress can work against you. And the moment it begins to work against you, then it's working for the opposition.

I've found that the best remedy for any kind of stress is to begin by identifying the reason you are stressed. Where exactly is the pressure coming from in your life? Sometimes this is easy.

You may be a writer faced with a tight deadline. You may be a student faced with a test. Perhaps your finances are not as good as you would like them to be and the bills are piling up and up. Or maybe you are in a relationship that is going nowhere. All of this is stressful, but not life threatening.

The first thing you have to realize is that you are not alone. Deadlines have existed since before the invention of the printing press. Students have taken tests for thousands of years. Bills have piled up for millions of other people. And as for relationships, well, they've been rocky since the Stone Age. Since time began, people have faced the same problems and have solved them. That is the whole idea behind support groups. You may not need a support group to get you through every little stressful situation, but it does help to know that millions of others have taken on the same problems and survived.

Your best weapon against stress is preparation. You shouldn't put added pressure on yourself by wanting to come up with an overnight solution to a complex problem. The answers to many of life's toughest challenges may take months or even years to work out. However, once you do come up with a course of action, you will feel better.

Even after you've prepared, trained, and strategized, there may still be some nagging doubts. We've all spent those sleepless nights, tossing and turning in bed, worrying about the future—whether the future's the next morning or the next ten years. A few years ago, someone brought me a poster of the classic Serenity Prayer: "God grant me the serenity to accept the things I cannot change; courage to change the things I can; and wisdom to know the difference." I have lived by that ever since, and I find it immensely comforting. If I can't control a situation, I don't even worry about it.

Fighters invariably suffer from short-term stress. I've seen fighters restless and edgy the night before a big bout. In twenty-four hours the fight will be over and they will have either won or lost, but the night before the fight is often sleepless. I've seen the same thing happen to friends before going into job interviews and also to myself the night before a multimillion-dollar contract negotiation. Some people get totally stressed out before their wedding, a big social event, or even a dentist appointment. But short-term stress is not a problem. It's the long-term stress that causes ulcers and heart attacks.

After all of the training and the preparation, when there is no more time, the best thing to do is not obsess about the job ahead. Instead, take your mind off it for a few hours. The diversion will allow you to relax and get much needed sleep. It doesn't matter whether you watch a movie or read a book. When out on the road with fighters, I'm never without my Scrabble board. I've played Scrabble hundreds of times with fighters, trainers, and cornermen the night before a big fight. You may prefer Monopoly or cards. The important thing is to take a little vacation from the tension that has been building for weeks or even months. The entertainment doesn't have to be event-oriented. Just cleaning the house, knitting, scanning e-mails on a laptop computer, or watching a little television can be great ways to relieve stress.

If you're stressed over someone's behavior, write her a letter. Just lay it on the line in the bluntest possible terms and then throw the letter away. The act of writing a letter and putting my feelings on paper not only helps me to better understand a situation but to relax as well. It allows me to vent my feelings. I am a firm believer in the power of the written word.

These diversionary tactics in no way take the place of training and preparing. If you go to a movie instead of training to meet a challenge, the challenge will still exist when the movie ends, and you will still be unprepared to meet it. There is a world of difference between taking a vacation from the stress and pressure that go along with a challenge and running away from that challenge. If you have good people in your corner, they should be able to identify stress when they see it, try to defuse it, and certainly not add to it. If you have people in your corner who are negative or dismissive, they can only add to the pressure.

The Stare-Down

The eyes are the windows to the soul. Why else have poets, writers, and singers exalted the beauty and power of the eyes for hundreds of years? Shakespeare wrote movingly of eyes; Cole Porter and Mick Jagger have both immortalized the eyes in songs. There's "Brown Eyed Girl," "Nancy with the Laughing Eyes," "Bette Davis Eyes," and many, many more. I consider my eyes to be one of my greatest assets.

I doubt, however, that a poet or songwriter will ever immortalize the look in a boxer's eyes when he enters a ring. A champion's eyes say, "I'm ready, I'm better than you, and I'm going to prove it as soon as the bell rings." Of course, that's a polite way of interpreting the look, because for anyone who has ever looked across the canvas to the opposite corner, the experience can be terrifying. It is said that early in his career Mike Tyson frightened most of his opponents into submission by the look he gave them before the first bell. Conversely, much was made of an incident several years ago when Vice President Dan Quayle lost his "game face" during a debate and acquired what reporters began calling a "deer in the headlights" gaze. Nobody remembers the question or the argument that seemingly frightened him. What they do remember is the look of fear in his eyes during the debate. A politician who shows fear in his eyes is dead at the polls.

In the boxing world, promoter/manager Don King has one of the most intimidating stare-downs in or outside of the ring. People tend to lower their eyes when speaking to him, never meeting his gaze. However, I've always met his gaze, making certain not to be the first to look away. I have found him to be charming and very clever. The same holds true for celebrities. Autograph seekers and admirers will often lower their gaze when approaching a celebrity. Looking away first can either indicate submissiveness or untrustworthiness, depending on the situation. By looking away, the person indicates that he is not meeting the other person on an equal level. This might be an unconscious response, such as with the autograph seeker, where lowered eyes might indicate respect. But more often than not, lowered eyes indicate a desire to hide something.

In our daily lives, eyes can not only help us master a situation but can relate important information. If you have ever seen a mother quiet an unruly child with "the look" or watched a woman in a bar turn away an aggressive man with one glance, then you understand. Aside from those casual instances, your eyes can be one of your most powerful tools when dealing with people, whether it be a social or a business setting. They can relate the entire gamut of emotions from affection to contempt. You can indicate your honesty and make your displeasure known without ever saying a word.

Very often we receive this information from others without ever realizing that we pick it up from their eyes. The next time you are in a situation where you can observe others easily, note the messages they may be sending with their eyes as well as with their body language. You will be amazed at the range of emotions and expressions that pass from one person to another without a single word being spoken.

Likewise, you should be very conscious of the messages you are sending with your own eyes. Very often the eyes are the first thing a person notices when he or she meets you and the first thing you notice. Someone who looks away, who doesn't meet your eyes, can make you uncomfortable without your even knowing why.

When meeting someone for the first time, you should absolutely make it a point to establish eye contact. Just as you would offer them your hand to shake, you should offer them your eyes. And you should take note if they do or do not return your gaze.

The Eyes Have It

Here are some of my favorite methods for using your "looks" to get what you want.

Angry Eyes

Angry eyes come in handy when you want to be a lady and don't want to make a scene. For instance, if you are in a store and a persistent saleswoman continually tells you how wonderful everything looks just to make a sale, it's time to fix her with an angry gaze. This glare will tell her, "Please stop hard-selling me. If I need your help, I will ask for it." If she has any common sense, she will get the message and walk away. Athletes have perfected the angry glare. They know how to use it and know how to recognize it when an opponent uses it. All of us have the ability to telegraph our anger with our eyes. It is a talent that can be developed. Simply think about why you are angry. Clench your jaw, knit your eyebrows together, and glare. The angry look will appear naturally.

Defiant Eyes

Defiant eyes are similar to angry eyes, but you don't have to be angry to feel defiant. When I am asked to do something I absolutely do not want to do, I flash my defiant eyes. What I'm saying is "No way!" The word "no" has always been one word that I avoid. I hate to be told that I can't do something or that I can't go somewhere. When I first started managing boxers, I was often treated like Cinderella's wicked stepmother. I had security men try to keep me out of my fighters' locker rooms, business associates try to bully me in meetings, and trainers act condescendingly to me in gyms. I found that it helped to stare them down defiantly. I found this tactic to be more effective than throwing a tantrum. Not only did it get my message across without words, but it left the door open to build mutual understanding without hard feelings. This is my "I mean business!" look.

Sad Eyes

When you are unhappy, grieving, or disappointed, it will generally show in your eyes. I have never been one to hide my feelings. When I am in a down mood, which is not very often, it is apparent. My eyes, which are usually bright, become flat and dull. It tells someone to be kind to me, I am having a bad day. If someone is unusually quiet and unanimated, look into their eyes. They may be unhappy about something. This is your signal to ask, "Is everything all right?" It may be just the opening they were waiting for, and they will open their heart to you.

Happy Eyes

Happy eyes shine and glisten. They radiate warmth and contentment. When things are going well for someone, it shows in his or her eyes first. A smile starts with the eyes. Have you ever noticed how some people put on a fake smile, but their eyes tell the real story? Their smile cannot hide the fact that they are not happy. When someone says something nice to me, I always say "thanks" first with my eyes. When I see someone I like, my eyes are bright and cheery. People's eyes are almost always happy around little children and animals. The whites of the eyes get whiter and the pupils seem more vivid. As we get older, the laugh lines around our eyes get more pronounced. I kind of like this since it accentuates happy eyes.

Seductive Eyes

These eyes do not necessarily have to be sexual, though that is certainly one way to use them. You can use your eyes to get others to do what you want them to do. It is a form of flirting.

Women have always been good at batting their eyelashes and act-ing coy. This look requires you to lower your eyelids and peek up from under them. Instead of sounding like a spoiled brat and saying, "Please, please let me have that!" I simply adopt a seduc-tive look that says, "You want to give that to me, don't you?" It's better to have something given to you than to have to ask for it. If you are trying to catch the eye of an attractive person you want to meet, a solid, unblinking look can open the door. Most people are taken aback by a frank, open stare. Never be the first one to break eye contact. Hold it until the other person looks away. It will give you the upper hand.

Devilish Eyes

This is one of my favorites. These dancing orbs tell people when you are up to no good or simply teasing. I have found that I can get away with a lot when my eyes relate the fact that I am not serious. These are the eyes that people see when you are being facetious, playful, or telling a little white lie. Some children are born with devilish eyes. You can take one look at them and know, "This little guy is a handful." With adults, it's very much the same thing. Certain people radiate an air of mischief. The class clown has devilish eyes. So does the practical joker and the life of the party.

Evil Eyes

When it comes to evil eyes, I think of Charles Manson. This man personifies evil, and it's all there in his eyes for the whole world to see. Criminals often have evil eyes. Their evil shows in their eyes, though they appear normal in every other way. Many boxers have evil eyes. Though they are not criminals, they have bad intentions. They make their money by intentionally hurting other men, and it often shows in their eyes.

Poker Eyes

These are a tremendous asset. They reveal nothing. No matter what you may be thinking or feeling, poker eyes will keep your secret. This is the hardest stare to develop. Since most people tend to telegraph their mood with their eyes, it is difficult to wipe out all traces of emotion. When I want to fix someone with a totally blank stare that reveals nothing, I try to think of a plain gray wall. I concentrate on that wall and my eyes go flat and void of expression. It becomes impossible for anyone to know what I have on my mind. I often use poker eyes during negotiations. This allows me to figure out where the other person is coming from while keeping them totally in the dark. A good boxer uses poker eyes during a fight to throw his opponent off guard. Whether he is hurt, tired, or even ready to fall, a clever boxer will show nothing in his eyes.

Loving Eyes

The best of all are loving eyes. These are reserved for special people and special occasions. When making love, cuddling, or holding your child, loving eyes are the way to convey your feelings. Pets look at their owners with loving eyes; brides and grooms look at each other with loving eyes; and parents watch their children walk down the aisle to pick up their diplomas with loving eyes.

So how does this help you in your day-to-day life? Very simply, by becoming aware of your eyes and your general appearance, you become more aware of the impression you are making on the people around you. It is only by controlling yourself to some degree that you can control a situation.

This does not mean that you should become an "actor" or a phony. What it does mean is to be aware of what you are saying with your eyes and body language. Women I know who would never wear a seductive dress into a business meeting for fear of losing credibility will sometimes give off the wrong signals with their eyes in the very same meeting. They won't make eye contact or will unintentionally flirt out of nervousness. They will undermine themselves and their positions without even knowing it.

When we learn how to read what others are saying with their eyes, we can react more effectively, whether we are dealing with a loved one, business associate, or friend. It always pays to learn the language of eyes.

TOUCH GLOVES AND COME OUT FIGHTING

I love the tradition of touching gloves before a fight. Both fighters are in the center of the ring, in neutral territory, while the ref explains the basic rules of the fight. He then asks the two fighters to acknowledge each other with a simple touch of their gloves.

Both boxers are usually so fueled with adrenaline that they can't wait to start the fight. They may be staring at each other with pure intimidating hatred, yet they quietly listen to the rules, usually touch gloves as instructed, and then move back to their corners to await the bell.

The touching of gloves is an acknowledgment and acceptance of the rules and parameters of the sport in which they're about to engage. It's a ritual that separates the spectacle of boxing from a common brawl. While the fighters are in the center of the ring, they may engage in some macho posturing and stares intended to rattle the other fighter's cage, but there is typically no show of uncontrolled temper or rage. Whatever its origins—probably shaking hands—touching gloves is a symbolic ritual that defines them as professional athletes who accept the rules of the sport.

Often you will hear a fighter denigrating his opponent in the media. He'll say, "He's a bum. He ain't about nothing." He does this primarily to psych himself up for the win. I encourage all of my fighters, regardless who they are fighting, to exhibit good sportsmanship and give their opponents the respect they deserve. They should respect the talent and hard work that put those opponents in the ring with them. Then, once they've won, they can take pride in their victory. They'll have the satisfaction of knowing they fought a clean fight and won it legitimately.

Sports fans will tolerate a lot: Dennis Rodman in a dress or the temper of John McEnroe, for instance. But they will not tolerate someone showing disrespect for the sports they love. Those fighters who belittle their opponents in the media or in the ring denigrate themselves in the process. If, for instance, the opponent is considered to be a bum, what does that make the fighters who belittle him? Why even bother to fight someone whose skills are so obviously inferior to your own? And, once you beat him, what was that victory worth? What is the value of beating a so-called bum?

I once managed a fighter who had a terrible attitude. Not only wouldn't he touch gloves before the fight, but he disparaged his opponents in the press and exhibited unsportsmanlike behavior when he lost—and even when he won. For a brief period he was seen as the "bad boy of boxing," but that didn't last. The fans got tired of his behavior, so did the press, the other fighters, and the refs. I can't speak for him, but I would say that he didn't respect the sport. He certainly didn't show it.

This applies to any job. If you've chosen the job carefully, planned your strategy, trained, and stuck to the fight plan, then why denigrate the accomplishment of completing it successfully? The executive who has just been made vice president of a division wouldn't say, "Well, who else would they choose? The other guys were all losers." It's always better to win over stiff competition than a pushover. It increases your own standing in the rankings and advances your career to the next level.

It's always smart to give people the respect they deserve, even if you're in competition with them. If anything, I tend to overpraise my competition. Respecting your competition doesn't mean you have to like him or her. It doesn't mean you have to be best buddies. And most of all, it doesn't diminish your fighting edge. If anything, it's a show of confidence. When a person goes out of his way to belittle the competition, it shows a lack of confidence. By respecting your competition, you're saying, "Okay, I'm not afraid of you, let's compete!"

It always makes you look good to be generous with your praise of the competition. It makes you seem smooth, confident, and on top of your game.

I've also always enjoyed the idea of the ref's instructions. Both fighters already know the rules of the fight; an experienced boxer has heard them hundreds of times before. Yet the ref always goes through the ritual of repeating these rules so that both fighters hear them at the same time. And always, included somewhere in the instructions, the ref asks for a "good, clean fight."

The ropes, the instructions, and the touching of gloves all combine to set the parameters of the match for both boxers— they are the golden rules of the sport. These are the same rules we should establish for ourselves in our own daily conflicts.

Love in the Clinches

Following are two lists of ground rules. The first one is for arguing with a loved one, and the second one sets ground rules for fights at work. They are very general but can keep a minor dispute from turning into a major fight. These rules work for me.

Ground Rules for Fighting with Your Spouse or Loved One

1. *No physical abuse or violence.* Absolutely none. Even smashing a plate in the heat of anger or slamming a door escalates the level of conflict to an unhealthy degree. If you've slammed that door or smashed that plate, apologize immediately to defuse the situation. This behavior is immature and destructive and sends a very bad message.

2. *Don't drink and fight.* Fighting after or during consuming alcoholic beverages is also a big, big no-no. After a couple of drinks, our senses are impaired and our emotions are often out of control. Remember, alcohol is a drug. Even small quantities may prompt us to say something we otherwise wouldn't say.

3. *Stick to the subject at hand.* If you are upset about a spouse not doing his share of chores around the house, don't change the

subject and start complaining about some other old issue. Stick to the current point. Don't dig up and rehash old issues.

4. *Be reasonable and logical.* If there is a problem, then state it in the most calm, reasonable fashion you can. Shouting, screaming, and hysterics never solved anything. Sooner or later you will have to discuss the problem and ways to solve it. It's better to avoid the aggravation and emotional stress by making that time sooner, rather than later.

5. *Don't attack, discuss.* Remember, the point of the discussion is to solve a problem, not inflict injury, even emotional injury. Name calling and other kinds of attacks do nothing to remedy a bad situation and only lead to hurt feelings that can linger for a long, long time.

6. *Listen.* Really listen to what the other person is saying . . . and ask questions. There is absolutely no rule that states you can't ask questions during an argument. I often stop in the middle of a heated discussion and ask the other person, "What did you mean by that?" or "And your point is . . . ?"

Ground Rules for Fights at Work

1. *State your case as clearly and logically as you possibly can.* Remember, the point of the conflict is to solve a problem, not to insult or belittle the other person. Good solutions often come from the exchange of ideas.

2. *Don't make it personal.* There is absolutely no excuse for attacking someone on the job. Treat everyone—from secretaries to the president of the company—as professionals. You can criticize a person's work performance without disparaging them personally. Abuse and ridicule can only make matters worse.

3. *Keep it private.* As much as possible, any confrontation should be discussed in private. Nobody likes to have their dirty laundry aired in public. If you are a supervisor who has a grievance with an employee, talk to him or her privately. The same is true if you are an employee who has a problem with your boss. By confronting someone in public, you run the risk of injuring his or her pride or undermining his or her authority. Even if he or she sees the logic of your arguments, he or she is less likely to back down or say that you are right in front of others.

Conduct yourself professionally at all times. Yelling, screaming, and throwing things is not professional in any business. If you want others to treat you as a professional, then you should act like one, particularly under pressure. Just as there is no excuse for a bully in the workplace, there is also no excuse for emotional dramatics. Both are unprofessional.

Setting the ground rules, of course, doesn't end the fight or resolve it. What it does is create an environment in which it is okay to disagree. In the same way that it is acceptable for two men to put on gloves, trunks, and step into a ring with the intention of fighting each other, it is equally unacceptable for those same two men to fight outside the ring. Whenever possible, level the playing field. Make sure that the odds are even for both sides.

Even though I'm a boxing fan, I've witnessed street fights and found them abhorrent. The difference between a street fight and a boxing match is the difference between night and day. And it's no different for any argument in which the ground rules haven't been set, whether it's at home or the office. Those fights, without ground rules, are the ones that are most apt to leave scars and bad blood. As long as both individuals know and accept the ground rules, then the chances for the fight turning dirty or spilling out into other aspects of their lives is greatly reduced.

For instance, a husband and wife should set rules they should try to follow—like making a deal that they will never go to bed mad, whatever happens during the day. They may not make love, not even cuddle, but they will be civil to each other. And the next morning, they will get up and wish each other a great day. It's not only easier, it cuts down on the stress. Going to bed with angry feelings is no impetus for a good night's sleep.

Another aspect of sportsmanship is the tradition of touching gloves when a fighter accidentally lands a low blow or head butt in the heat of battle. When this happens, a sportsmanlike boxer will reach out his glove and touch the opponent's in apology. It's the way that he acknowledges a mistake.

Even in conflict, we should acknowledge our mistakes and low blows. It's just good behavior. It can also head off a retaliation of low blows from our opponent. By acknowledging a misdeed and apologizing for it, we reconfirm the rules of the conflict. It's like saying, "The rules still apply."

Playing by the Rules

Fighting dirty is a short-term solution that very often comes back to haunt us. Here is my list of rules to follow for civilized conduct every day:

Ground Rules for Civilized Conduct

1. *Treat everyone with respect and dignity.* The woman cleaning your hotel room or office should be treated with the same courtesy you would treat the owner of the hotel or building. Remember—a year from now that person may be in a wonderful new position, and she will remember how nice you were when she was still struggling and unknown.

2. *Don't take credit for someone else's work.* Give credit where credit is due—and expect the same from those around you. Don't claim an idea as yours when you know very well that someone else came up with it first.

3. *Never discredit someone else to make yourself look or feel better.* This is a major problem with some women: They will endlessly criticize another woman's makeup, body, or intelligence. This behavior does nothing but make anyone who engages in it look unkind and petty. And remember, often what goes around, comes around again.

4. *Don't make a big issue out of every little thing.* We live in an imperfect world, and problems arise every day. Why waste your time and energy complaining about insignificant things? Those who complain about every imperfection or mistake eventually are not heard, even when large problems arise.

5. *If you don't have something nice to say . . .* Try not to say anything about a person you wouldn't say to his or her face. Negative comments have a way of getting back to people. They also make you look petty.

6. *Be generous.* Pick up a check every once in a while when it's not expected. Put change from purchases into the charity cans at local stores. You'll feel better about yourself when you start thinking about others.

7. *Smile at people.* When approaching anyone with whom you're about to speak, smile. Again, you'll feel better, and you'll make her day a little brighter.

8. *Don't talk down to people.* When you "talk down" to someone, you are disrespecting them in order to make yourself feel better. In almost every instance, it doesn't earn you an ounce of respect and very often creates hard feelings. Never be condescending.

9. *Take a moment to compliment someone.* If the boss has a new suit that looks great, tell him or her. Do the same for the clerk at

the local store or the guy in the mailroom. I make certain that I give out at least three compliments a day. It's not hard to find something nice to say to almost everyone you see. It puts a smile on people's faces, and they love you for making them feel good about themselves.

10. *Be polite.* Use the words *please* and *thank you* generously. It's just basic courtesy. Appreciate it when people are nice to you and acknowledge it.

11. *Admit when you are wrong.* We all make mistakes. It's a tough thing to do, but if you're going to take credit when things go right, then you have to take blame when they go wrong. Add the words *I'm sorry* to your vocabulary—they're important. If you feel uncomfortable saying that, handle it in a humorous way. For example, I may turn to someone and say, "Can you believe I just did that! What a ditz I am today. I certainly didn't mean that."

Into the Center of the Ring

How you enter a situation is absolutely crucial. I don't care if you're entering a party, your boss's office, or the boardroom of a Fortune 500 corporation. Walk into the room with confidence—not cockiness or false cordiality—but looking as if you're prepared for whatever awaits you in that room. Project an air of confidence and people will give you respect instantly.

Chances are that you worked hard to get into the ring. If you've been following the advice in this book, then you are prepared for it. So now that you have a chance to "punch with the big boys," why undermine yourself and "build up" your opponent's confidence by entering the fight with the attitude of someone destined or expecting to lose? If you learn only a few tips from this book, make this one of them. When entering a situation, go to the center of the ring to meet your opponent, touch gloves as if you knew you were destined to win the fight, and then come out slugging.

There are two fights where this approach really stood out. The first is when Muhammad Ali took on George Foreman in Zaire in the "Rumble in the Jungle." Ali was an extreme underdog. Hundreds of so-called experts said he didn't have a chance against his bigger and stronger opponent. Foreman was a hard-punching fighter, perhaps the hardest puncher ever. Everyone assumed that Ali would try to dance and bob and weave his way around Foreman. Some even speculated that his strategy, if he ever got a chance to enact it, would include "running." During the fight, Ali did bob and weave and exhibit some remarkable moves. But when the bell rang, he was out of his corner and aggressively moving to the center of the ring toward Foreman, attacking the larger, stronger man.

Obviously, this was a moment that Ali had trained hard for and was part of his overall strategy. But in moving so aggressively toward the center of the ring, he showed his opponent that he didn't fear the heavy blows that every expert said would devastate him. By the end of the fight, Foreman was exhausted and Ali triumphed.

The same held true for the first Evander Holyfield/Mike Tyson fight. Again, every expert said that the biggest obstacle facing Tyson was that he had to be sure to set his alarm clock to get up in time for the fight. However, when the bell rang, Holyfield, unlike many of Tyson's previous opponents, leapt at the champ from his corner, aggressively meeting him in the center of the ring.

Both of these fighters nearly ran to the center of the ring to touch gloves against opponents that all of the so-called experts said they couldn't beat. They were showing their opponents that they were more than ready to start the fight. And in those few seconds when they touched gloves, went to their corners, and then came bounding back, they wiped away everything the experts said.

They showed that they were ready and prepared . . . and perhaps even planted a small seed of doubt in the other guy's mind.

Obviously, the office isn't the same as a boxing ring. And certainly a cocktail party isn't the same as a championship fight, at least not the ones I attend. You don't want to enter these situations too aggressively, but you do want to enter with self-confidence. People can make judgments in an instant. First impressions are important; you don't get a second chance at them. Someone who stares at the floor, hunches his shoulders, or fidgets with his hands shows not only that he lacks self-confidence but that he's a person on the defensive. And there is no telling how people will react to that. Sensing what they perceive as weakness, they may go on the attack. In business situations, particularly negotiations, this is deadly. People are much less inclined to make concessions to someone they sense as weak or without bargaining power. Or, sensing a defensive attitude or weakness, they may choose to just ignore that person. This is particularly true in social situations. Think of the stereotype of the wallflower. She may be seen as shy or introverted, but rarely is she approached, except perhaps briefly by the host or a few friends.

I know this advice may go against natural tendencies. Some of us *are* shy and not very aggressive in the best situations. However, this is something that can be worked on, and something that can be practiced. Start with people you know in social situations. Make it a point of greeting them before they approach you. Then begin practicing with people you know less well. It will seem strange at first, perhaps a little awkward. It may even feel *fake*. However, as you develop your own style, you'll begin to notice how the expressions of those you meet change. Their smiles will become a little broader, their reception a little warmer, and they will take you more seriously.

Confidence is a magnet. People are attracted to those who exude it. It is the power of suggestion at work. When a person acts as though she has everything under control and is on top of her game—that is the way people perceive her. If you practice it enough, it becomes natural and easy. Eventually, if you do it enough, it becomes your reality. You are confident. You can easily walk into a room of strangers and set the room on fire with your presence.

People are attracted to winners. They are attracted to them in the same way they are attracted to beauty. Whatever situation you enter, whether it's part of your daily routine or brand new, you should walk in a winner. Prepare for every threshold you cross in life, and then stride through it with confidence.

There are times when the center of the ring is the only place to fight, such as when interviewing for a job. Remember, if you want to win, you must prepare your strategy in advance. You have to step through those thresholds confident and prepared to meet whatever awaits you on the other side. A true winner rarely approaches a situation unprepared. It's perfectly natural to be nervous. I don't know a single intelligent person who isn't nervous from time to time. However, what is unnatural among smart people is being caught off guard.

The mistake that so many people make, time and again, is not knowing when they've entered the ring in the first place. They simply aren't paying attention. They may be at a vitally important meeting at work, but they doze through it because they treat it like it's only another in a long line of useless meetings. Or they may be at an office social event where they drink too much and make a fool of themselves.

So, remember, there isn't always a ref around to tell you when to touch gloves and come out fighting.

Plan Ahead to Get That Job!

Dress appropriately. Obviously you wouldn't wear casual clothes to a job interview. The way you dress communicates important messages about you. Find an opportunity to see how the firm's employees dress ahead of time. Don't walk into an interview in a flashy designer suit if the corporate culture of the firm is conservative. Walk into the interview looking as if you belong at that firm. This, of course, depends on the situation. Some jobs call for a person to dress interestingly and stylishly. Jobs in the fashion and art industry allow more freedom of dress than corporate positions.

Go beyond your resume. Enter that interview with a mental list of skills and experience that you would bring to the firm that are not on your resume but will pleasantly surprise the interviewer. During the course of the interview, bring up a story that illustrates your skills and creativity. Give examples of ways that you are a team player, get along with coworkers, and are willing to work hard.

Make and hold eye contact. Look the interviewer in the eye. This can sometimes be difficult because you're nervous, but do your best.

Smile. Yes, smile when appropriate. This may be harder than it sounds, but listen carefully and smile when the interviewer says something that might be amusing. A smile can send a message of poise, self-confidence, and friendliness.

Compliment the interviewer. Don't overdo it, but find something nice to say about the person who interviews you. It might be a comment about his colorful tie or the furnishings of her office, but find something nice to say, even if it is a simple comment about the company. Make the interviewer feel that you really want to work there.

Give them a reason for hiring you. Go into the interview with at least two good reasons why you want the job and why you are perfect for it.

Ask questions. The interview is a conversation. Just as the person behind the desk is trying to find out about you and your qualifications, you should be trying to find out about the company. The questions you ask should show off your knowledge of the company and its services or products. These should be positive questions, however, regarding the company's recent expansion, new line of products, or some other success. Think of one or two questions to ask as you do your research into the firm before the interview. Negative questions, such as, "How is that lawsuit against you going?" or "Is it true that the president of the company was indicted?" are obviously out. Also, questions about benefits and vacations should be asked at the appropriate time. The right time to ask these questions is either after the personnel manager broaches the subject or toward the end of the process, after you have been offered the job. Questions regarding benefits should not be among the first you ask during an interview. Think of the interview as a "first date" where you are both trying to get to know one another.

Do your homework. An interview, like a boxing match, requires preparation. You should never go into an interview without researching the company and its products. A good general rule to follow is to always know more about the company and their products than they know about you.

LEARN TO BOB AND WEAVE

Until this point, I've focused primarily on offensive tactics—those moves that will help you deliver the knockout punch. Just as important, however, are the defensive tactics. A smart opponent simply doesn't stand at the center of the ring waiting to get punched. Just as in boxing the fighter bobs and weaves to avoid punches, in our own lives we should try to avoid as many unnecessary hits as possible. After all, they're unpleasant and they don't help us win.

We all know people who are "catchers." Hopefully it's not physical abuse but some other "hit" that they've taken again and again. They are the employees at work whose bosses hurl horrible and demeaning insults at them or the women who accept put-downs from their spouses or boyfriends. Usually these people get our sympathy, but little else. They are generally not respected or admired. We usually say, "She's hanging in there," or "I can't believe he took that."

Oddly, after a while we don't even ask why they are taking those "hits." We're so used to them being berated, cheated, or otherwise treated badly that we see it as part of who they are; it becomes part of their personality and their identity. We even stop questioning why they stand still for it. They become victims.

Inside the ring, catchers are not respected as much as skilled boxers. Outside the ring—in real life—the very best that they can hope for is sympathy from friends and coworkers. And after a while, that sympathy inevitably turns to pity. Soon their friends and coworkers—even the people in their corner—expect them to lose. They might even expect themselves to lose. It's a natural part of life to receive some hits and low blows. It's even natural to lose once a while. But there is absolutely no sense in anyone making himself a target in life or in the ring. Don't get so used to losing that you come to expect it and accept it.

One of the all-time greatest fighters dates back to the eighteenth century. His name was Daniel Mendoza, and he is generally credited with turning boxing from a sport in which opponents stood toe to toe and beat the daylights out of one another into a thinking sport. He was, quite frankly, the first person in boxing to ask the question: "Why do I have to be hit all the time? There must be a better way." For a sport that has existed for thousands of years, someone might have asked the question sooner, but the sport has a history of changing very slowly that is still true today.

As the story goes, Mendoza emerged victorious but badly hurt from his first professional fight. He immediately took a leave from the ring and spent the next three years perfecting his method of bobbing, weaving, and guarding himself. His first opponents didn't quite know what to make of his unusual tactics. Some critics at the time called him cowardly for his strategic retreats and for using his agility to avoid blows. For the vast majority of the press and fans, however, he eventually emerged as a hero. He had not only advanced the sport of boxing from a bloody spectacle to an actual sport but posted win after win, until he was finally declared the champion of England. After retiring, he passed his knowledge on to others, becoming an esteemed boxing coach.

Mendoza's techniques, though refined through the years, are still in use today by champions all over the world. Mendoza showed the world that there is no glory in accepting unnecessary punishment—a lesson many people should learn outside the ring as well. However, remnants of the pre-Mendoza age continue to thrive. There are fighters who are known as catchers because they tend to catch far more blows than they deliver. They're willing to suffer the pain and injury to wait for the perfect time to deliver their punches. Not only do these fighters endure far more pain than necessary, but they generally have shorter careers and lose more fights than they win. As every smart fighter knows, there are enough unavoidable blows in a fight. There's no sense in taking more than is absolutely necessary. For this reason, a smart fighter will train hard and prepare strategies for avoiding as many punches as possible.

Bobbing and weaving is much different than running. A runner is often a fighter who has not prepared, has panicked, or is just outright scared of his opponent. On the other hand, every-one admires the ability to bob and weave. It's a skill that makes the smart fighter look good and makes his opponent look bad. A fighter who can successfully bob and weave out of the way of his opponent not only saves himself needless pain but can actually frustrate his opponent into making what could prove a costly mistake.

The fighter who bobs and weaves demonstrates a mastery of the art of boxing that is not lost on the crowd or the judges. It shows that he's spent time practicing and preparing. He's facing his opponent, he isn't running, and he's facing him in a smart way. He avoids the powerful blows that could potentially knock him out and simultaneously protects himself against the small jabs that will eventually sap his strength and throw his coordination off.

In everyday life, the ability to bob and weave is the ability to identify problems and potentially problematic situations early on, and then move out of the way. A perfect example of this is having to deal with a spouse who arrives home from work in a bad mood. Ideally, in these cases you can go to his corner and offer advice and encouragement, but sometimes this isn't possible. Often, the best you can do is simply stay out of the way and not provoke him. You can either avoid the subject or deflect it by changing it.

We all bob and weave every day one way or another. I've learned to spot the moods of those closest to me, and it's safe to say that they've done the same around me. If someone makes a negative comment, I can't allow it to become an issue. Taking every comment, every remark personally will only scatter your energies. It will wear you out, leaving little strength for the big fights. I let small negative comments made by those around me pass. I always consider the source, the mood, and the circum-stances.

Bobbing and weaving is an absolutely essential skill in busi-ness. From the time you interview for a position until you leave the company, you are bobbing and weaving. In the business world, bobbing and weaving does not mean avoiding work or stabbing those you work with in the back. What it means is accentuating the good and the positive in your work and solving problems creatively.

In my business, for instance, I am constantly going into negotiations with some very tough executives in the sports and entertainment worlds. These are men and women who are the best at what they do. They know their business and very often know the boxing business. When I confer with them, it's with the understanding that we are there to divide a "dollar pie" between my boxer, the opponent, and their venue or television network. It is what is called in business a zero-sum game. Very simply, this means that there are only so many dollars in that pie. The more I get, the less they get, and vice versa.

In reality, this is the heart of negotiating: dividing a pie. It might be a dollar pie you divide with your boss or company; a time pie you divide with your spouse or loved one; or a work pie you divide with your coworkers. More often than not, someone wins and someone else loses. Very rarely is the pie divided equally.

At each of these meetings I attend, the executives might have mentally prepared a list of reasons why my fighter should get less than what I want him to get, and less than what I think he deserves. They may question the poor attendance at his last fight or that the odds are running against him. It is my job as his manager and negotiator to be able to answer these questions—not lie, but answer each of these questions truthfully while avoiding negative impact on my boxer's pay. For instance, if the attendance was poor at his last fight, I have to know why and be able to communicate that. Perhaps it was raining the night of the fight. The fight may have taken place the same night as the World Series or the day of the Super Bowl.

I am not lying, nor am I offering excuses. By having the facts on hand, I am able to offer explanations for whatever negatives they throw at me. And I also have my own list of facts. Perhaps the fighter has a record of 20–0 and the kind of winning momentum that can take him to the championship. Perhaps this future fight is with the only opponent he never beat—making the bout something of a "grudge match." These are explanations, not excuses. Many people confuse the two. True, sometimes they are similar in that they allow you to avoid a negative situation. Here is a very simple rule of thumb: An excuse is what is said when a mistake or an error has occurred. It is a way to defend an inferior position. An explanation is what is said when you want to bolster an already strong position. It reinforces your point.

Another way to bob and weave is to downplay the negative and accentuate the positive. Think of this tactic as you would think about dressing for a date. Whether we like to admit it or not, even the most enlightened woman (or man for that matter) will buy clothes that accentuate her or his best features. The woman with great legs is naturally drawn to shorter dresses and skirts. The woman with a slim waist will tend to dress in a way that displays that attribute. I personally don't think there is anything deceptive or shameful in this. People naturally want to show themselves off in the best and most appealing way. You do it for the person you are dating, or for your spouse, but you also do it for yourself. When you look better, you feel better about yourself, and others respond to you in a more positive manner.

The same is true for all of life's negotiations, large and small. Whenever you go into any situation, think of the best arguments at your disposal along with your weak points. Then decide how you can neutralize those weaknesses with positive points.

Like everything else, there are right ways and wrong ways to bob and weave. Fighters who go through their careers trying to avoid all blows rarely win. Why should they win? Their entire fight plan is getting out of the way of the other guy's fists, with little thought given to how to win.

We all know people who spend their entire lives doing nothing but bobbing and weaving. They are the ones who always lay low at work so that they are almost invisible. They are the constant joke tellers or worse, the "yes men." Very often they are either charming or harmless, but in almost all cases, they are not winners and certainly not champions because, when the going gets tough, on the job or in their personal lives, they can be counted on simply not to be there. As every fighter will tell you, to win you have to show up.

In real life, bobbing and weaving should be a creative defense. In boxing, it entails the fighter quickening his reflexes and learning the right moves so that he is already evading the punch before it's even thrown. To bob and weave successfully in real life, we have to not only be aware of those around us but use our creativity to develop strategies for dealing with difficult situations.

When I was still in high school, the Rolling Stones made their first U.S. tour. I was a freelance journalist and knew that an interview with the Stones would score big points with my editor and get noticed nationally. But it was the height of the British Invasion, and Mick Jagger was already a major sex symbol and bad boy of rock 'n' roll. Every journalist in Detroit—in the world!—wanted an interview, and only a precious few were getting them. My press pass got me backstage for the show, where it was near-chaos with groupies, hangers-on, and lord knows what else. What could I do to compete with the kind of attention they were getting?

Somehow I managed to work my way through the crowd to the band. They were only a few years older than I was at the time. Jagger and the others were young, far away from home, and looking a little lost. So I invited them to dinner at my house. The next thing I knew, we were sitting around my kitchen table as if we were high school friends, talking and eating my mother's delicious lamb chops.

I got the interview, which to this day still puzzles many journalists. Recently I picked up a history of the Rolling Stones that mentioned that memorable dinner. Whenever anybody calls the

Rolling Stones the band of "sex and drugs and rock 'n' roll," I always add, "and don't forget lamb chops."

Bobbing and Weaving Is

1. Avoiding unnecessary or unproductive conflict.

2. Using your powers of reason, even when others may not be using their own.

3. Giving up an unimportant or small point to make your own larger point.

4. Refusing to be sucked into a fight that you can't win.

5. Looking at the big picture, not just at the immediate situation.

Bobbing and Weaving Is Not

1. Lying to gain an advantage.

2. Running away to avoid all conflict in your life.

3. Practicing deceitful low-blow tactics.

4. Making excuses for your own actions.

5. Justifying behavior you know is wrong.

WATCH THOSE LOW BLOWS

In life, as in boxing, you're going to get hurt every once in a while. Friends will disappoint you. Your career will suffer some setbacks. Lovers will leave. And even the best-thought-out plans will go awry. No matter how rich, successful, famous, or beautiful you are, there are going to be some tough times, disappointments, and failures every time you step into the ring. And that's okay. Perfect fights are few and far between. You certainly won't be thrilled by every setback and disappointment, but you shouldn't let them keep you down, either. Even in the boxing world, the fighter who has been knocked out with a single punch eventually gets up, brushes himself off, and goes back into training for the next fight.

In boxing, a low blow is a punch below the belt to a particularly sensitive area of the male anatomy. However, what really hurts are the low blows that come our way outside the ring. These can include infidelity by a lover or spouse, the loss of a job, even a vicious rumor. How many times have we heard about a husband having an affair with the wife's best friend? Almost as familiar are the stories about the hard worker who gets passed over for the big promotion by the unethical officemate. These are classic low blows. To make matters worse, a low blow can come at any time and from any direction, frequently when we least expect it and are unprepared. These strikes against us wound us particularly because they were so unexpected and darned unfair.

Words can wound us almost as much. Vicious gossip can be devastating. After all, when the unfaithful spouse takes up with the best friend or the unethical coworker plays dirty, at least those around you see the wrong that has been done. Gossip, however, can be even more insidious and hurtful since the true victim is often seen as the villain. For instance, if someone spread the rumor that you had an affair with your spouse's best friend or used unethical tactics to get a promotion, as ridiculously unlikely and untrue as those rumors may seem, there are people who are always willing to believe the worst about you. Unfortunately, for many people in our lives—coworkers, friends, acquaintances, and even family—there is not much difference between gossip and fact. An unproven or untrue suspicion is enough to hold against someone.

Sadly, the ones who are most hurt by low blows are often those who play by the rules. If you agreed to play by the rules by touching gloves, you should expect the other person to also play fairly. Obviously, this is not always the case, inside or outside the ring. We've all had experiences where adversaries have started unpleasant rumors about us, intimidated us, or tried to discredit us. There are literally thousands of low blows in life, and they can all wound us to a greater or lesser degree. For women, the added threat of sexual harassment can be the lowest blow of all. It not only undermines a woman's dignity but can impact her professional standing. And because of that, it can hurt twice as much.

In the ring, a fighter who is on the receiving end of a low blow has a choice. He can either shrug off the punch and wait for the referee to see the violation in the rules, or he can start fighting dirty as well. The right thing to do is to wait for the ref to call a foul and continue to fight cleanly. Realistically, that's not always as easy as it sounds. After receiving a low blow, you're often hurt and angry. Every instinct tells you to retaliate in kind. After all, the other person started it. Who could blame you if you fought dirty in return? You may even have people in your corner or the audience urging you to fight dirty, just to teach the other person a lesson.

In boxing this hardly ever works. In fact, it very often fails, and actually reduces a fighter's chance of winning. It also demeans him, even if he does win the match. Responding to a dirty fighter by retaliating in kind forces a boxer to deviate from his fight plan. The second he starts fighting dirty, he begins fighting in the other person's fighting style, which could be unfamiliar or might leave him open to a clean punch. Even if the ref didn't see the illegal punch his opponent delivered, he might see the one the fighter returned, and the fighter could lose points.

There's no glory in winning a dirty fight. It marks a fighter as less than professional, and future opponents, if they have the least bit of dirty fighter in them, won't hesitate to punch low when facing him. The minute a fighter throws a low blow, he loses credibility in the eyes of the boxing world. Suddenly he has become a dirty fighter who can't win a fair match. This may not seem to mean much, but ultimately it could prove devastating to a fighter's career. Opponents won't want to face him in the ring, the judges who sit ringside will watch him closely for the slightest infraction of the rules, the press will minimize even his clean victories, and the fans will turn against him because he has not shown the proper respect for the sport.

Perhaps the lowest of the low blows occurred in the second Holyfield/Tyson fight. Even those with no interest in boxing heard about Mike Tyson biting Evander Holyfield's ear. The jokes began almost immediately. Yet there was nothing funny about it. In just a few seconds, Mike Tyson not only brought shame to the sport—eliciting a sense of disgust among his peers and the entire boxing world—but besmirched his own reputation forever. There is an excellent chance that those few seconds of foul play will remain with him forever, tainting past accomplishments and future achievements. Even if Tyson had been knocked out, he would still be remembered for his past brilliance in the ring, but he discredited himself in a way that Holyfield could never have done, even with the most spectacular knockout in boxing history. And he did it in a fight that Tyson might still have won.

In real life, the same principles hold true. For instance, take the case of office gossip. A vicious, untrue rumor could be circulating about you. If you know who started the rumor, you could decide to strike back with a rumor of your own. Doing this immediately brands you an office gossip, no better than the person who started the original rumor. In fact, it may even add credibility to the rumor he or she began. A better option would be to confront the person civilly, either alone or in front of others, informing him or her that the rumor isn't true.

Then there is the case of the unfaithful spouse or lover whose damaged reputation means he or she will have a much tougher time gaining the trust of future lovers or spouses. That is to be expected. In addition, once word gets out, he or she may also be seen as untrustworthy in other areas of their lives, such as business. Following is a checklist for the lowest blow you can deliver to a loved one—cheating on him or her.

To Cheat or Not to Cheat—Is It Even a Question?

- His or her spouse will find out.

- The person with whom he or she is having the affair will turn out to be even more demanding than his or her spouse.

- He or she will sacrifice too much money or time to keep the person happy.

- He or she may have to eventually choose between spouse and lover.

- The tension and stress caused by deceit may have adverse effects.

- He or she may contract a sexually transmitted disease (STD).

The smart person will consider all the possible negatives before getting into a situation like this. And just think of how much heartache and deception could be eliminated if everyone studied the possible consequences before becoming involved in an affair. The same holds true for virtually every major decision we make.

The best way to deal with low blows is to avoid them entirely. If a particular person is known to be a gossip, for instance, then avoid gossiping with him or her about other people, and for heaven's sake, don't confide in him or her. If someone is known to be unreliable, don't rely on that person. If a male worker is known to be lecherous, then don't flirt with him. This isn't as easy as it sounds. Often the worst gossips are the most charming. Cheating lovers are often goodlooking. And the most devious coworkers appear the most professional and helpful. It's easy to let your guard down in the heat of the moment, and worse, it's easy to ignore your instincts.

The worst thing we can do about a low blow is not to prepare for it. It's very easy to ignore all the warning signs. After all, we'd all like to live in a perfect world, where everyone follows the rules. Sadly, this just isn't the case. Ignoring the bad doesn't diminish its impact one bit. It's easy to convince ourselves that because we play by the rules, we should ignore the bad. This is precisely how we leave ourselves open to dirty tricks. Then, after the blow has been struck and we're hurt, we're disappointed that the ref or audience didn't see the transgression. The refs in the ring are good but not perfect. They do miss the low blows sometimes. The same is true in everyday life. Injustices are done and nobody gets caught.

Many of us make the mistake of ignoring the warning signs. Yet, if you've done the research, you can prepare for the low blows and protect yourself. You should note in particular if your opponent is known for throwing low blows and then formulate your fight plan accordingly. If the company has a reputation for layoffs or a high rate of staff turnover, if your lover has a reputation for cheating, and if your friend has very few "old" friends, then that should signal there is something wrong. If avoidance doesn't work, the next best thing is to bob and weave around the low blows. However, no matter how well you research your adversary or how well you prepare, those low blows will still sneak in.

When I first entered the all-male world of boxing, I had to deal with all kinds of harassment. Some of it was joking "old-boy" stuff, and some of it was downright mean-spirited. I knew that if I were to succeed in this profession, I would have to deal with it effectively and in a way that wouldn't make me more of an outsider. I could have responded to the worst of these insults with the same kind of crude language thrown at me. I could have devastated those Neanderthals. And it would have felt good, but only temporarily. Ultimately, I would have done myself more harm than good, so I chose to deflect the insults with humor. Without being insulting or getting flustered, I made it known that the comments weren't appreciated. In the more mean-spirited instances, I simply sidestepped the blows by not reacting. Sometimes I gave the perpetrator a look that told him I didn't find his behavior humorous. It was important that I didn't show that I was hurt, however. Showing weakness in those situations is often an irresistible temptation for the offenders to strike again. Naturally, there are limits. In cases of sexual harassment, the moment a boss or coworker interferes with your ability to perform your job, it's time to start thinking in terms of more serious actions. The second they touch you in an unwanted manner, you must bring this to the attention of your supervisor or your human resources department.

All's Fair in Love and War

Here's a checklist that I've devised of key traits to look for when contemplating a long-term relationship or even marriage. I've avoided making value judgments in most cases. After all, who is to say whether it's better to be a "night person" or a "day person"? However, when a night person starts dating a day person, it could lead to real trouble. Neither one is likely to surrender his or her old ways easily. The more you have in common with a person, the better the odds are of the relationship succeeding.

Essential Romance Checklist

Past history. Has this person been married or engaged before? What went wrong? A friend of mine started dating a fabulous forty-year-old man who was rich and never married. After a year of serious dating, she finally approached him about marriage. To keep her quiet, he bought a ring. After another year, without setting a specific date, she discovered he had been engaged *seven* times before and never set a wedding date with any of his previous fiancées, either. Under pressure, he finally broke up with my friend, making her the eighth ex-fiancée. Had she known about his history of engagements, she never would have let the relationship drag on as long as it did. It was his pattern, and he repeated the same behavior over and over. Each new woman fell for his charm and promises without knowing that he had made and broken engagements again and again.

Professional matters. What is this person's educational and professional background? Does he or she drift from one job to another or from one college to another? This can tell you a lot about the person's ability to make a commitment.

Family matters. Is the person from a large family, or is he or she an only child? (I once dated an only child and found that he was spoiled and not very good at compromise.) Regardless of whether he's an only child or from a large family, pay attention to his relationship with his family. Some people telegraph their behavioral traits.

More family matters. Are his parents still alive? It is said that the way a man treats his mother is a good indication of how he treats women in general. By the same token, a woman who was raised as "Daddy's little princess" will expect the same high-maintenance treatment from all men.

Children in the future. How does this person feel about children? It never ceases to amaze me how many people get married without discussing whether they want to have children. And whenever I hear a woman say, "I never really believed that he didn't want children," I know I'm listening to someone who hasn't done her homework. Never consider a long-term relationship with someone without discussing all the important life issues.

Personal tastes. Find out the kinds of food, movies, music, and sports this person likes. Okay, this is first-date conversation, but it's important: It can help you decide whether there will be a second date. It can also be a good indicator of the type of person you're dating. A person's taste can reveal a lot about his personality. For instance, the forty-year-old who loves teen slasher movies and heavy-metal rock bands might prove a little immature for a long-term relationship. Mutual tastes in food and music can also provide valuable touchpoints in a relationship. It's horrible to discover later that you have nothing in common with the person you're dating, then have serious conflicts about where to go or what to do every time you plan to go out.

Day person or night owl? Is the person a day person or a night owl? It isn't much fun being dragged out to clubs at midnight when your usual bedtime is 10:30 P.M. Likewise, the early riser who loves to stay home with a quiet video and climb into bed before midnight won't provide the social stimulation needed to keep the late-night social butterfly happy for long.

Athlete or couch potato? How athletic is the person? Someone who plays golf, tennis, or racquetball daily won't consider the couch potato much fun in the long run.

Affection. Does he or she like to be touched? Face it, some people are touchy-feely types, and others are much less demonstrative. I have a good friend who loves being touched and cuddled and kissed, while her husband is not demonstrative at all. They have fights about this all the time. She curls up next to him as they watch TV and strokes his back. He never returns the gesture, and when she complains about it, an argument ensues.

How well do they argue? Is the person aggressive or passive when it comes to arguing? Some people hate confrontations, and others can't wait to air their grievances in the open. Nothing is more annoying to the other than confronting their opposite in a fight. I am a non-arguer. My personality does not allow me to yell, scream, and argue. When I am faced with an argumentative person, the disagreement never lasts long. I listen, I state my point, and then I walk away. The other person is left standing there yelling at the door.

Sometimes the fight isn't fair. I'll tell you what they never told you in school—*the world isn't a fair place.* Bad things happen for no apparent reason. Everyone doesn't play by the rules. People with highly regarded qualities such as sincerity, intelligence, and honesty often go unrewarded, whereas those who possess the exact opposite qualities seem to succeed.

Yes, there is racism, sexism, ageism, and a thousand other *isms* that hold us back or block our progress. Some people are born smarter or better looking or into a life of material comfort, whereas others seem to have every conceivable obstacle thrown in their path. I could name thousands of ways in which life just isn't fair. But we aren't playing on a level field, and if we sit around waiting for the world to fix itself, then we'll have a long wait indeed.

The world can be a horribly unfair place, and we should all work to make it better in our own way. The way someone deals with life's unfairness is what separates a true champion from a loser. The loser will always find an excuse for losing; the champion will find a way to win no matter what obstacles he or she faces. We shouldn't use the obstacles thrown in our path as excuses to fail or to quit. When someone points to the unfairness of a situation as a reason to give up, he is accomplishing the one thing that no opponent could ever hope to do: knocking himself out before the first bell. He hasn't even given himself a fighting chance to succeed. We shouldn't be victims; rather, as people who have overcome adversity, we should be role models.

A few years ago there was much talk about how we were becoming a nation of victims. Television talk shows and magazines were filled with stories of people who had been victimized in one way or another. Some of these people had undergone horrible ordeals that certainly deserved our compassion and prayers, and others presented claims that were obviously frivolous. What struck me about these people was that in almost every instance, they had not only accepted but had also embraced the role of victim. It was how they defined themselves. They had let themselves become completely overwhelmed by whatever tragedy had befallen them or whatever obstacle had blocked their progress.

We all know people like this in our own lives. They are the ones who come to us with a problem, asking for our understanding and sympathy. When we offer them sympathy, it's readily accepted, but when we offer a solution to the problem, they rebuff it almost immediately. If people have problems, then sympathy from those in their corner is fine, but solutions are even better.

Every true winner and every champion I know has the ability to get up after the worst defeat, no matter how unfair, and keep going. It isn't easy. He may feel hurt, angry, and humiliated, but he keeps going. The people that I really admire are those who have found a way around life's obstacles. They are the ones who met life on its own terms and through perseverance, ingenuity, and talent found a way to succeed. The sports superstar born with natural talent was recognized early and was given the attention and training to nurture his talent. He is certainly thrilling to admire in action. No less so the handicapped student, who has overcome seemingly insurmountable odds to finish her academic degree with honors.

To win, you have to at least acknowledge the drawbacks of the situation in which you find yourself. Sometimes these are your own shortcomings, and sometimes they are circumstances built into the situation. Either way, there is no such thing as a perfect situation; every job or relationship you begin will include its share of obstacles. Once you acknowledge them, you can begin planning a way to overcome them.

I entered a business that had seen few woman managers before. I was able to turn that significant liability of being a woman in a male-dominated world into an asset. I used my training in public relations to get press for my fighters and myself. I used the curiosity of promoters about a woman manager to get my foot in the door and then dealt with them as a professional. I acknowledged the shortcomings of the boxing world going into it—and never looked back. Boxing was the arena in which I had chosen to make my career, and I knew that I would have to accept it on its own terms. I was determined to succeed despite whatever narrow-mindedness I encountered along the way. From the beginning, I entered the sport to become the best manager in the business and to represent my fighters to the best of my ability. I wasn't in the sport to change attitudes, though I suspect I did a little of that as well.

Granted, in all the years I've been in the business, I haven't changed the world of boxing dramatically, but I have managed to carve out my own little place in it. I succeeded in it to a level that many men never reach. There were times when the blatant unfairness of it all seemed nearly overwhelming, but I didn't give up. Boxing is a tough sport, inhabited by tough people, and I had to become just as tough if I wanted to do the job well. It is a business in which weakness of any kind can be interpreted as a fatal flaw, and I was tested again and again. If the business negotiations were brutal, then I determined that I could be just as brutal. If the atmosphere was inhospitably sexist and macho, then I wouldn't shrink from it or show weakness. Perhaps the women who follow me will have an easier time of it; perhaps not. I took on the challenge using my brains and ingenuity.

What is true in the insular world of boxing is true in the outside world as well. Very few businesses are as ruthless as boxing. Yet as women continue to make progress in the workplace, they are encountering much of the same narrow-mindedness that I came up against when I entered the sport. The best advice I can give them is to change what they can and to use their ingenuity to figure out a way around those obstacles that can't be changed. Meet the world on its own terms.

Two of the most important lessons I have learned are that you can't please everyone and that you will never be liked by everyone you know. I used to try to win over each person I met, and I hoped that they would think (and speak) highly of me. I found that this is a total impossibility. No matter how hard you try and how nice you are, there will always be people who dislike you for one reason or another.

HIT ME WITH YOUR BEST SHOT

Life deals all of us tough breaks: low blows and bad situations that are virtually impossible to avoid. Sometimes they catch us by surprise, and other times we see them coming. Either way, they can still knock us for a loop. Long-term loving relationships can and do end badly. Careers take downturns. Jobs disappear. These are the unpleasant and often painful facts of life. They may not be fair and most certainly will pain us in some way, but they are part of all of our lives at one time or another.

We all know somebody who is quick to say get up, brush yourself off, and move on. This usually doesn't help matters much. When life knocks us on our butts, it's hard to get up and continue as if nothing has happened. We're in pain, perhaps even confused about what exactly happened. After a bad experience, none of us is in the mood to get up and continue as if everything is fine. However, the way we deal with the tough breaks determines how successful we are in the future. Sometimes just as one door closes behind us, another one unexpectedly opens. I know that sounds clichéd, but it's true.

I haven't welcomed the hardships that have come my way, but I've tried not to complain about them. To the best of my ability, I've worked hard to accept the tough breaks and move on. In many instances, I know they helped me to overcome obstacles that came my way later. The best way to deal with life's letdowns is not to pretend they didn't happen but to salvage something positive out of them.

First, there are two basic kinds of bad breaks: those we can anticipate and those we never see coming until it's too late. We can prepare for the first kind. A smart fighter always wants to know his opponent's best punch. If an opponent has a devastating left hook, there's a good chance that sometime during the fight, regardless of how long or hard he's prepared, he's going to get hit with a left hook and it's going to hurt. For a fighter who prepares properly, that punch will not be a surprise. Oh, it may hurt like hell, but anticipating it will help him deflect the blows or brace for them.

I always want to know the worst-case scenario of any given situation. Like the old saying goes, "Hope for the best but prepare for the worst." In business, this is absolutely essential. All business deals begin with the best of intentions, yet very often the smallest detail can send an entire enterprise into a tailspin that leads to hard feelings or worse—lawsuits. Each time I make a business deal, I study both the best possible result as well as the worst imaginable outcome. Once I know and understand the worst possible outcome, then I can begin to prepare for it. The moment I've acknowledged that possibility, I've already begun the process of minimizing its effect. This thinking isn't negative, it's simply realistic.

However, sometimes you might find yourself in a situation that you couldn't have possibly anticipated. For instance, the dream job that turns into an office nightmare because the person who hired you decides to leave the company, or the attentive lover who turns out to be a cheater. Episodes like these leave you hurt and resentful, yet, with a little creative thinking, it is possible to carry something positive away from these situations, or even turn them completely around.

I remember when one of my fighters, Boom Boom Johnson, fought a particularly tough opponent. Johnson was the World Featherweight Champion at the time. He was a good fighter with good preparation, training, technical ability, and heart. He was simply outboxed for several rounds and was in bad shape. By the eleventh round, he was tired and a bit dazed, and he left himself open for a terrific blow to the jaw. He went down, but by drawing on some reserve of heart, he was able to lift himself to his feet again. Fortunately, he was saved by the bell and managed to stagger back to the corner.

Frankly, anyone in the audience that night would have counted him out for the twelfth round. That last punch seemed to take all the wind out of his sails. Then his trainer said to him, "That's as bad as it gets. That was his best shot and you're still standing!" That's all Boom Boom needed to hear. The trainer was right. His opponent had landed a perfect punch, and Boom Boom had gotten up off the canvas. A few seconds later, the bell sounded to begin the twelfth round, and Boom Boom went back into the ring and won the fight. He'd seen the worst his opponent could dish out, and the worst didn't end the fight for him. Boom Boom's trainer, like many trainers, was a master of psychology. With just a few words, he turned that devastating blow from defeat into victory. At a time when some fighters would have been looking for an excuse to throw in the towel, Boom Boom found an excuse to go back into the center of the ring and win.

You should take what you have learned from the tough fights of one situation and apply them to another. Suppose you're given an assignment by the company president to compile a detailed report in a very short period of time. No doubt it's a tough assignment. There isn't much time, and the report has to be perfect. Why panic? You've handled tough assignments before. There was the project for the division manager six months before, and another assignment from a vice president last year. At the time, those assignments seemed overwhelming, but you managed to do them. You've already been there and done that, and, more important, you survived.

The German philosopher Friedrich Nietzsche once said, "What does not kill us makes us stronger." I say, "What doesn't knock you out puts you in a better position to win, either the current fight or the next one." You can learn something from a bad situation that can help you overcome either present or future obstacles. No fight is ever completely lost as long as you have learned from it and can apply it to your advantage in the future.

A friend of mine once took a job with a large corporation. For the first six months everything was fine. She brought in more business than ever for the company and performed better than anyone had ever performed in her position. Then one of her superiors felt threatened by her outstanding ability. Suddenly she found her budget for the department cut back, every aspect of her work closely scrutinized, and her successes within the company minimized. Her superior made her life as unpleasant as possible. Just when things seemed as if they couldn't get any worse, the company announced that her department was merging with another division, and she was out of a job.

For a brief time she was devastated by the news. It seemed as if all of her hard work over the previous year had been for naught. The bright future that she was promised with the company when she took the job was now history. But she didn't let it depress her for long. Within a few weeks of moving out of her office, she met with former customers and set up her own business, at first out of her home, and then, later, in office space of her own. She even received a few job offers from former customers who appreciated her expertise. Two years earlier, she wouldn't have dreamed of going into business for herself. She lacked the experience that the large company had afforded her, and she didn't have the credibility that her former employer gave her. She would not have been able to get her foot in the door with those customers had she not first taken the job and then lost it.

Most people don't like to dwell on the negative. I understand this mode of thinking entirely. It's unpleasant at best. It's so much more enjoyable to think happy, positive thoughts all of the time. But this is simply unrealistic, not to mention dishonest. If you see a problem on the horizon, immediately prepare to deal with it. Ignoring a problem can turn a manageable situation into one that is devastating. You'll be surprised how that solid punch doesn't hurt quite so badly once you've prepared yourself for it. Oh, it will still hurt, you can be sure of that, but it won't send you out of the game.

If you can take your opponent's worst shot—be it an insult, a piece of office treachery, or a put-down—and it doesn't knock you out, then you've won the fight. *Always* get a feel for what the worst-case scenario holds in store for you. Let your mind go there. Think of the worst that can happen, and you'll be surprised that it isn't as bad as you thought. By allowing yourself to think of the worst, you immediately begin to defuse it. Don't let it frighten you; let it motivate you to action, even if it is a defensive action. Think of a new training regime that will cover the worst-case scenario, or figure out a way to avoid it altogether. At the very least, you've already mentally prepared for the blow.

At the same time, it is important not to exaggerate an unpleasant situation. We all know people who are in a perpetual state of despair. Everything and everyone around them is horrible. Their jobs are horrible, their relationships are horrible, their social lives are horrible. This attitude is just as destructive and unrealistic as perpetual happiness. By seeing only the negative, people who feel this way make themselves blind to opportunities that may present themselves, and they see themselves as victims. Once they cast themselves in that victim mode, they decrease their chances of winning in the future. Just as Boom Boom's trainer justified his ability to win the fight, victims are forever justifying why they lose.

For the vast majority of people, life is neither entirely horrific nor entirely happy. It is a combination of both. Be prepared to take the good along with the bad. The next time you encounter a friend who sees only the bad and none of the good, ask him what he's done to remedy the situation. Nine times out of ten he will shrug his shoulders and say, "What can I do?" This type of person goes through life seeing only the low blows and the hard punches. He doesn't prepare, he doesn't analyze his situation, and worst of all, he very rarely fights back. He can detail every personal or professional setback he's ever encountered. But ask him how he fought back or what he learned from these setbacks and he will probably come up blank.

When my mother died in my arms in 1996, I was devastated. I had lost my best friend and confidante. Several months later my father suffered an irreversible stroke and had to be put in a nursing home. During this same period, my husband of thirty years walked out. I was shaken and noticeably wobbly. But I managed to keep standing and go on with my life. I took the shots and continued the fight.

Recovering from Those Best Shots

When I watch one of my fighters in the ring, I often know exactly what his opponent's best shot is, and so does my boxer. It may be an uppercut or a jab or a straight punch, but we've reviewed the tapes and know the worst that a particular fighter can dish out.

When you get hit with an opponent's best shot, you go through a series of emotions. The first might be surprise. The sheer power of the blow is enough to stagger you. Perhaps you've seen the same thing before, from a distance, but experiencing it firsthand can knock the wind out of you. Many of us have had this experience with divorce. Experiencing it from a distance is nothing like experiencing it firsthand, and nothing can fully prepare you for it. Still, if you've readied yourself for it mentally, then it's far easier to recover. Just knowing that those tough hits are going to hurt like hell helps you deal with them. Yes, the intensity can be a surprise. They can leave you disoriented and a little stunned. But right then is the time to remember that you're still standing and have resources at your command.

Another common emotion is disbelief. After all, you trained hard and worked hard. How did that punch get through your defenses? In the ring, there's no getting around the fact that you've been hit. Outside the ring, there is always the temptation to deny it. Sometimes you can deny it by simply not acknowledging that you've been hit. Other times you can run away from the fact. Drinking, taking drugs, and other destructive behaviors are some of the ways that people attempt to run away, but none of those things work. Ultimately, everyone has to acknowledge what happened. If you don't, you leave yourself open to making the same mistakes again and again.

After receiving an opponent's best shot, you might feel anger. In the ring, becoming angry is one of the worst mistakes a fighter can make. A fighter blinded by rage and the idea of revenge makes mistakes. He forgets the fight plan and strategies that he so painstakingly developed and refined through training. He may even forget some boxing basics. A boxer's rage can often be his opponent's best weapon. By surrendering to rage, he very often leaves himself open to more punishment. If his opponent landed a lucky punch, the enraged boxer leaves himself open for his opponent to make the best possible use of his skill to deliver even more blows.

Outside the ring, anger can be equally devastating. The enraged employee who has just been fired is tempted to "trash" his office, tell the boss "what he really thinks of him," or even steal something from the company. These things may feel good at the time or satisfy some need for revenge, but they actually work against the employee. Those feelings that demand revenge are better put to use creatively. For instance, go to work for a competing firm and become an asset there. It's best to channel that energy—and it can be sizable—from something negative into something positive. The best fighters—the champions—let those feelings of revenge motivate them to fight harder and smarter.

A fighter who can take an opponent's best shot and not go down for the count or have it affect him negatively has won a major advantage over his opponent. The ability to come back and act as if that punch was nothing more than a love tap shakes his opponent's confidence to the core.

Dealing with Those Hard Hits

When faced with a problem—large or small—write down a list of possible solutions and potential consequences. For example, a woman who discovers a lump in her breast has several choices:

1. Ignore it and hope it's nothing.

2. Monitor it herself for a few months and see if it changes.

3. Go to a doctor immediately and have a mammogram.

If she selects the first option, she must realize that the worst possible outcome might be a malignancy that goes undetected for too long. If she opts for the second choice, she runs the same risk but only slightly improves the odds in her favor. Although the third choice may confirm her worst fears, it increases her chances of surviving if she discovers it's cancer. Of course, the smart choice is the third, but you can only know this by studying the alternatives. The same is true for almost any decision you make. The consequences of each possible course of action will dictate the right decision for you. I've gone through it three times and took an aggressive approach each time. One resulted in a biopsy; one resulted in a lumpectomy; and I'm still watching one. I decided that a proactive approach to a problem is the best. Meet the challenge head on and don't waste time.

Win or lose, a good fighter walks away from every fight having learned something about himself. We should adopt the same philosophy in our own lives. Often our toughest fights teach us the greatest lessons. When we walk away from a fight untouched, we know we've applied the skill and knowledge learned in the past. But when we receive those hard blows that life hits us with, we should see them as opportunities to analyze and discover what skills we need to build on. Granted, those are hard and painful lessons to learn, but very often they are the most valuable things we take from life. We also learn that we are able to withstand more than we thought going in, or we can overcome an obstacle that we thought was insurmountable. We took on the challenge—took the best shot—and lived to tell the tale and learn from it.

Giving It Your Best Shot on the Job

Even doing your job well is no guarantee of success. Fair or not, appearances in an office count. As someone once said, "If you don't blow your own horn, then there won't be any music." Following is a list of what you can do to become a standout employee.

Tips for Job Success

Arrive early. Make it a point to get to work early every once in a while to get a jump on the day's work. Not only will you accomplish more that day, but you'll reinforce the boss's impression of you as an ambitious worker.

Stay late. Likewise, make it a point to stay late once in a while.

Be generous. Bring in a box of chocolates or cookies and set them out on your desk for other employees. More important, be generous with your time. If a new employee needs help finding his way around, then offer to show him the ropes. Giving of yourself is still the ultimate gift you can give to someone else.

Neatness counts. Keep your work area neat and clean. Before you leave at the end of the day, spend a few extra minutes putting your work area in order. It will make you more efficient in the long run. At times my desk gets so cluttered that I waste valuable time looking for a particular piece of paper. I finally devised a desktop filing system that keeps all my papers at my fingertips.

All work, little play. Keep personal calls or personal computer time to a minimum. Even when passing by a cubicle or office quickly, it is easy to tell when someone is engaged in work or play. Use work time for work and play time for play.

Avoid gossip. Gossiping or arguing with a coworker is an obvious no-no, but everyone needs to be reminded of it every so often. Remember: the person who is the first to start a rumor is also usually the first to complain to the boss about his coworkers.

Remember where you are. Remember that you are in a place of business, not a social club. That's not to say you can't be friendly or make friends, but your number one goal should be to perform your job as efficiently and effectively as you possibly can. In many instances, the friendships you form on the job will not last beyond the workplace. This is a sad but true fact of life. When people leave a job, there might be a going-away party or dinner, with promises to "stay in touch," but rarely are these promises kept.

Read, read, read. When you first get the job, find the trade journal for that industry and read it cover to cover. Go to the library and read back issues of it for the past year. These trade journals provide valuable information on industry developments as well as the major players. The information you receive from these periodicals will not only quickly establish you on your current job but will provide a good resource for finding your next job.

Avoid office romance. Few businesses or industries look kindly on office romances. And few office love affairs remain secrets for long. Sooner or later the word will spread through the organization and possibly through the entire industry.

Creating that incredible, indelible credibility. Face it, some people are just more credible than others. Walter Cronkite, the newscaster, was beloved by millions because he was credible. People believed what he said and trusted him to tell the truth. Women in particular face credibility problems, both on and off the job. If a woman comes up with a solution to a complex problem, it is often likely to be questioned before being implemented.

In this respect, boxers have it easy. They simply have to get into the ring, fight, and win. They are judged on the quality of their opponents and the number of wins they have. Nobody can subtract those wins from their record or discount their importance. In this way, the ring is so much more fair than the office or a social setting, where people may judge a person on perceptions and not accomplishments.

I faced this kind of credibility problem when I was first starting out in the sport. Naturally, I was prepared, but even that wasn't
enough. The immediate assumption many of the cigar chompers made when I first appeared on the scene was, "What can a
woman know about boxing?" Well, actually, I knew quite a bit,
but whatever I said didn't count for much because I was thought
of as a "dame," a "broad," a "skirt," and quite a few other less
nice terms.

What I did was set about creating credibility for myself. Rather
than try to imitate the cigar chompers' style, I created my own
style within their world. Following are a few of the tips I picked
up along the way. Remember, this advice is not meant to replace
preparation, the fight plan, or strategy, only enhance it.

Helpful Tips to Assure Credibility

Be serious. If you are in a serious situation, act in a serious manner. Avoid joking, flirting, or other diversions. Focus on the job at
hand. It's nice to be liked, and joking and flirting are ways you can
accomplish this, but there are simply some situations where being
liked is beside the point.

Dress appropriately. The guys may say you look great in that
short skirt, but it's not appropriate at a business meeting or con-
ference. You may get their attention, but you won't gain their respect.

Focus. Make whatever you have to say short and to the point
when dealing with superiors in a business setting. If you have a
question, don't apologize for asking it. Ask the person to clarify
or restate what he or she said. Never say, "I don't understand."

Problem? What problem? Avoid going to your superior with a
problem you expect him to solve. If you have to go to him with a

problem, propose a solution. He may modify it or suggest another solution, but you've counterpunched any notions he may have had of you as a "totally helpless female."

Don't complain. I don't care if it's a killer case of PMS or a broken nail, never complain to your superior about it. And besides, a fifty-year-old male vice president is in a poor position to offer any solutions to either problem.

Think it before you say it. Know exactly what you are going to say before you say it. Avoid fumbling for words or stumbling over facts.

Don't try to be one of the boys. Yes, some women can pull this off. It's been my experience, however, that most can't and shouldn't try. Cursing, drinking, and commenting on other women's anatomy either comes off phony or is seen as strictly a novelty act by male coworkers.

Don't be afraid to fight. Don't shy away from a confrontation when you know you are right. But be sure to keep it strictly professional and fight by the rules.

If you don't know, then don't speak. Nothing is more valued than expertise. At the same time, nothing will lessen a person's credibility more than providing wrong information. We all know loudmouths who claim to be experts on everything from computers to cars when in fact they know very little about either. One of the keys to developing credibility and respect among your peers and coworkers is the value of your opinion. Although everyone has opinions, ones that are based on hard-earned knowledge are rare indeed. When you offer your opinion only when you're absolutely certain, you'll become known as a source of reliable information.

You Can Run, but You Can't Hide

There's a humorous saying that goes, "No matter where you go, there you are." I could add to that and say, ". . . and your problems are there with you." Nothing could be more true.

In boxing, the ring is a stark, brightly lit square of canvas surrounded by ropes and marked by four posts. There is nothing between a fighter and his opponent except empty space. That is one of the more fascinating aspects of boxing. Each opponent is forced, by virtue of the playing field, to face his opponent head-on. There is literally no place to hide in the ring. The fighter has only two options: fight or quit. It is senseless to try to retreat because there is no place to retreat. The fighter faced with an opponent who is stronger, more talented, and better prepared can move from corner to corner and side to side. He can retreat until he has tested every corner and every inch of rope that surrounds him, but the other guy will still come after him. He will either begin fighting or quit.

Fighters who retreat are called runners. To be called a runner in boxing is the ultimate insult. Running is seen as an act of cowardice and as an act of futility. Running is worse than being beaten. A runner loses the respect of not only his opponent but the crowd, the ref, and the judges as well.

In our own lives, there is often the illusion of being able to run away from a bad situation or count on some unexpected outside source for help. There are no ropes or a precisely measured square of canvas marking the boundaries. We are able to retreat into offices and rooms where we can close doors. We can jump on airplanes or into our cars and put miles between ourselves and our problems or opponents. We can buy a lottery ticket and hope that luck is with us. But for all the good it does us, we might as well still be in a twenty-three-foot ring surrounded by padded ropes and four posts. Even when they know that, many people faced with a seemingly unbeatable problem still try to escape by running. They go on vacations, relocate, quit job after job, change spouses, or escape into alcohol or drugs. But the problem is still going to be there.

You can run from the unpleasant realities of life until you spend all of your time doing nothing but running, and those realities will still catch up with you. And when they do catch up, you will realize that all the time and effort wasted in running could have been used preparing and planning. Obviously, in cases where there is an abusive spouse or a relationship at work, flight is a form of fighting back. It's a way of simply not taking on the fight. There is absolutely nothing wrong with removing yourself from a fight if the opponent is not following the rules of the game or if you are so unevenly matched that you have no hope of winning. But in far too many cases, the urge to flee takes hold when the fight is winnable.

Preparation

Assuming you chose your fight carefully, then it's up to you to face it to the best of your ability. If there is a problem, it is always better to face it. The first step in facing it and coming out on top is preparation.

The fighter who is about to take a step up in his career by going against a champion may start running long before the bell for the first round is sounded. One of the most common methods of running is denial. The fighter scheduled to go up against a tough opponent will begin denying the problem he faces from the moment the fight contract is signed. He will deny it by overrating himself and underrating his opponent. Consequently he doesn't train as hard as he should. He doesn't develop a clearly defined fight plan and doesn't bother to assemble a winning team in his corner. For all his bravado, he'll face an opponent who is better prepared, better trained, and better managed in the ring. The outcome is predictable. He may have been running for six or eight months outside the ring by denying the seriousness of the situation. Once he is in the ring, however, the opponent's skill, preparation, and training are seemingly insurmountable problems. It's then that the fighter begins running again.

Sadly, with the proper training, the right attitude, and preparation, the opponent might have presented a problem—perhaps even a large one—but the fighter at least had a chance of winning. By denying the problem, he also denied himself any chance of victory. He ran and ran but ultimately couldn't hide from either the opponent or the inevitable loss.

Identify Your Problems

The first step any fighter takes before a big bout is identifying problems he may run into. He knows the fighter he will be facing. He knows whether the fight is for the championship and how many rounds are in the fight. He also knows how long he has to prepare for the fight. Then he'll define his opponent's strong points and weak points and form his strategies for training and for the fight itself. He faces the problems head-on, studying them from all angles in search of possible solutions. He doesn't do this alone; he works with his corner to help develop his plan. The fighter and his corner face the problems together. As the fighter prepares, a wonderful thing happens. The opponent becomes more and more beatable. The fighter may still lose, but he's put the odds in his favor by accepting his opponent's skill and planning for it before he has to step into the ring.

Joe Louis, one of the most famous boxers in history, was the champ when he was knocked out by Max Schmeling. A winner of twenty-seven professional fights, his defeat by Schmeling shocked both the audience and the media. Schmeling's style was technical, whereas Louis's was a hard-punching approach to the sport. Rather than accept defeat, Louis launched himself into training. He fought a series of bouts that not only earned him a chance to regain the title but allowed him to practice against more technical fighters. When at last he faced Schmeling again for the championship, he scored a knockout, and in record time. There could be little doubt that when he reentered the ring, he had trained and prepared and was ready to regain his championship title.

Fighting Against Yourself

One of the toughest fights most people take on is the fight against themselves. And sadly, a lot of them lose. They can't run from themselves any more than they can run from their problems with the outside world. Just as a boxer who may be in denial over the quality of the competition he faces, people may deny their own problems. The most obvious example of this is substance abuse. But even smaller problems, such as dealing with weight, appearance, or lack of education present sizable obstacles for many people.

My advice is the same that I offer my fighters before a big bout. This is the guy we signed on to fight. Now evaluate, prepare, and face him in the ring. Simply stated, you fix what can be fixed, and what can't be fixed you try to minimize. Before a boxer enters the ring, it's absolutely essential that he feel good about himself. The way he does this is through preparation. He's fixed what could be fixed, whether it's his speed, style, strength, or fight plan. The fighter who steps into the ring feeling horrible about himself and his abilities will get nothing but agreement from his competition.

For women, especially, this is a trap. If you don't like your hairstyle, change it. If you're a few pounds overweight, create a plan to lose them. Do what you have to do to feel good about yourself. Nothing is ever as difficult as you think it will be. After you prepare and form a strategy, you'll be surprised how the largest tasks become less daunting. My advice to my friends and fighters is "go for it." But go prepared. Go for it with the proper preparation, with a strategy, and with the confidence needed to win. There are women who truly feel horrible about their appearance. They may avoid social situations, fade into the background at work, or simply shut others out. All that wasted time and potential is simply a shame. Most of these women have exaggerated their unattractiveness. They lack willpower and have just given up. They are running but staying in the same place. By comparison, if feeling heavy is the problem, it would be so much easier to lose a few pounds. Changing their diets and starting modest at-home exercise programs would not only improve their outward appearance but do wonders for their self-confidence.

I hate to say it, but women may be the worst runners. From early on, we've been told not to compete with men, not to seek and never to participate in conflict of any type. Consequently, women often don't prepare. They don't form a fight plan, they don't train, and they don't expect to win. And, quite frankly, why should they expect to win? They don't deserve to win. They have done none of the things that all winners—all champions—have in common. In many instances, these women will blame everyone except themselves for their own lack of preparation. They will deny their responsibility.

Jealousy

In addition to denial, if you don't feel good about yourself, you may fall victim to jealousy—one of the most common signs of insecurity. It's also one of the most useless and harmful emotions. It weakens your position in other people's eyes as well as your own. Jealousy is a natural emotion. If your husband or lover looks at another woman, you can feel the jealousy pop to the surface. Yet when it does, you're giving something to her and taking something away from yourself. Yes, there are women who have perfect legs, perfect breasts, and perfect butts. There are women who graduate Phi Beta Kappa and design rockets for NASA. And there are women who run multinational corporations. We all have friends who are prettier or smarter or more successful than we are. My answer is a resounding, "So what?" There is always some advantage that we have over them. We each have our own special qualities and talents. The trick is to develop them as much as possible, although this is not as easy as it sounds. We can be our own worst enemies when it comes to recognizing and developing our best qualities.

It often amazes me that the same women who can spot the good qualities in others—both physical and intellectual—have such a difficult time recognizing those same qualities in themselves. They can spot a beautiful woman from across a crowded room and feel jealous, yet up close, looking in a mirror, they fail to see and appreciate their own beauty. They will marvel at someone else's wit or intellect, yet never acknowledge their own. Frankly, these women are deceiving both themselves and others. It's a deception that does them absolutely no good whatsoever. They are portraying themselves as less than they are or could be. The phrase "brutally honest" is often taken to be negative. Well, if these women were brutally honest with themselves, they would see that they are far smarter and prettier than the women of whom they are jealous, and they would feel positive instead.

To a large extent and to an amazing degree, it really does all equal out. Try the following experiment if you don't believe me. Privately, make a list of the women of whom you are jealous. No movie stars or sports figures or public personalities, please. You don't really know them, so leave them off this list. Being brutally honest, list their best attributes on one side of the piece of paper. On the other side of the paper list their shortcomings. Be absolutely honest. Now do the same for yourself, only add an additional section headed "potential." This potential section could include everything from losing ten pounds to going back to school for a degree. Undoubtedly, after comparing the two lists, you will have other women beat hands down—and even more so after taking into account the potential column.

The Daily Grind

Going through daily life is like getting into the ring. You're either prepared or unprepared for the day ahead. If you're like me, you face a hundred challenges and problems each and every day. These aren't huge championship bouts but rather small conflicts, which, when added up, can wear you out and drag you down for the big fights.

We all have friends who constantly seem overworked, overwhelmed, and in over their heads. And we also have friends who are always cool, collected, and calm. Often there is very little difference in their lifestyles or the challenges they face. The difference between the two is how they go about meeting those challenges. At one point in my life I was tasked with raising my sons, writing for a newspaper, doing TV interviews, and hosting my own radio show. I also ran a public relations firm, and I used to hear people refer to me as a "superwoman." I never thought of myself that way. I just believed that I could do it all, and I found a way to fit it all in without exhausting myself. It was a matter of time management, high energy, and a desire to get the most out of each day.

Following is a checklist and guidelines for taking on the day-to-day battles we all face in our homes and careers. They are very basic, but you'll be surprised at what a difference they can make if you follow them for only a short period of time. You will find that you function more efficiently and that you have energy to spare at the end of the day.

Don't Knock Yourself Out: Part One

When someone tells you to "knock yourself out," it usually means they recognize that you are about to embark on some useless or overstrenuous task. Following is a short checklist intended to help us weed out those tasks from our daily lives. Please note, this is not a list of excuses to avoid important but unpleasant or demanding work; rather, it's a list to eliminate strictly unnecessary work.

- ☐ How important is the job?

- ☐ Who benefits most by your accomplishing this task?

- ☐ List at least three reasons for taking on the job in the first place.
  1. _____
  2. _____
  3. _____

- ☐ Do others perceive the job as a waste of time?

- ☐ If others do see it as a waste of time, then why do you perceive it as important?

- ☐ Are you the best person to do the job?

Don't Knock Yourself Out: Part Two

Once you take on a demanding task, it can seem larger or more challenging than it actually is. Often a person makes the work much more difficult by not working smart. Following are very general guidelines on how to work smart and efficiently.

A perfect recipe. If the task or job is complex, list its different steps and the items required to accomplish the task. Write this list as you would a recipe, with the different ingredients at the top and each step in order at the bottom.

Research beforehand. Research any aspects or steps you may not fully understand. For instance, if you are driving a troop of

Cub Scouts to a campsite, then map out your route before starting. If you are building bookshelves, then make a dry run to the lumberyard and ask questions regarding the types of wood available and their different qualities.

Set a schedule. You wouldn't put a pie in the oven or recaulk the bathroom without knowing how long each task took to complete. Likewise, this schedule should allow you plenty of time to complete the task as well as accomplish the other items on your list.

Prepare for mistakes. Even the best cooks, carpenters, or fighters make mistakes. They are inevitable. However, you can limit the number of mistakes you make by listing possible problems before you begin. Some of these you can eliminate just by identifying them—for instance, removing the backseats from the minivan before driving to the hardware store to pick up that new bathroom fixture. For other problem areas, being aware of them will act as a warning to you to pay extra close attention when carrying them out.

Do you have the right people in your corner? If you run into a problem, do you have someone you can call in an emergency for advice or help? For instance, if the new computer you just bought doesn't "boot up," will the salesman who sold you the system be available to answer questions on the phone, or do you have to call the manufacturer? My advice: Ask the salesman if you can call him if you have any problems with the setup, but keep the phone number of the manufacturer handy, just in case.

PEOPLE WITH GLASS JAWS SHOULDN'T . . .

A fighter is said to have a glass jaw when he is susceptible to injury. Glass is brittle; it breaks easily. A fighter's glass jaw is his Achilles' heel. Achilles was the Greek warrior in Homer's epic who was impervious to injury anywhere on his body except for his heel. Of course, the moment the Trojan enemy learned of his weakness, they immediately aimed their arrows at Achilles' heel.

All of us, like Achilles, have a weakness. The best fighters in the world have at least one weakness. The way they deal with this flaw in themselves is first by recognizing it, and then by training to strengthen themselves against this weakness. They will also adopt a style that allows them to avoid blows to a weak area. This might involve covering up a glass jaw by positioning their body or arms in a special way, or learning to artfully bob and weave around their weakness.

Take note of your own particular weak points. First, seek to improve them. You can do this through training. If your job requires you to use a particular software program at least part of the time and you can't seem to master it, then force yourself to train harder on it rather than avoid the program. Take a refresher course, if necessary. Second, adopt a fight plan that will limit the number of blows that you receive to that area. For instance, if someone in your workplace is known to bed more than her share of men, it would be ill-advised to gossip about her, especially if your own private life can't stand up to close scrutiny. As the old saying goes, "People who live in glass houses shouldn't throw stones."

Once you take on a fight, be it competition for a job, a political maneuver at work, or competition for a spouse, you should be aware of your own weaknesses or shortcomings just as much—if not more so—than those of your opponent. It is absolutely essential to remember that the type of fight your opponent wages against you depends, in part, on the type of fight in which you engage. If you gossip in the workplace, then be prepared to be gossiped about. If you maneuver behind a boss or coworker's back, then expect the same in return.

I've always found it ironic in my business dealings that the type of person who engages in such practices can least afford to have those same tactics turned against him. The loudmouth who is always criticizing others is very often the most thin-skinned. The gossip who carries stories around the workplace is the one with the most checkered past. And the braggart who boasts about his own ability is inevitably the least competent.

The golden rule in boxing is that to throw a punch, you have to be willing to take one back. All of us would do well in our day-to-day lives to remember this. When you attack someone, be it a spouse, a lover, or a coworker, how many "unanswered blows" do you think you can throw before that person strikes back? You may be genuinely angry—mad as hell at that person—but if you want to throw insults, you should consider just how long that person will take before he says something mean to you.

Remember, words are like punches thrown in the ring—you can't take them back. If you can't take what you dish out, then don't dish it out. It's as simple as that. It amazes me how those who show the least sensitivity to the feelings of others are often overly sensitive themselves.

Advice for People with Glass Jaws

1. If you like to tease others, be a good sport if someone teases you in return.

2. If you're going to criticize others in either their work or personal lives, then be prepared to accept criticism from those around you.

3. If you tend to accept others' hospitality or generosity freely, be certain you offer it just as freely to them.

4. If you are doing something illegal, immoral, unhealthy, or unethical, don't criticize others for doing the same thing.

5. Don't tell people that they are doing something the wrong way unless you can explain to them how to do it the right way.

6. Don't tell people that their kids are rude, lazy, or otherwise indulging in bad behavior unless you are certain your kids aren't doing the same things.

7. Don't flirt unless you're willing to accept your spouse or date flirting as well.

KNOW WHEN TO THROW IN THE TOWEL

We all lose sometimes. Muhammad Ali, Mike Tyson, and George Foreman have all lost fights. The biggest movie stars have made flops. The smartest executives have made bad business decisions. And almost everyone has been in a relationship that didn't work out. Nobody can win all the time. Life is just not like that.

Faced with the choice between winning and losing, I always choose winning. On the other hand, throwing in the towel doesn't mark you as a loser for life. Naturally, you don't want to make a habit of quitting when the going gets tough, but there is no shame in taking yourself out of the competition when the situation is impossible. One of the most painful sights in boxing is watching a fighter keep fighting well beyond any chance of winning. At that point, boxing becomes something less than a sport. You may admire the boxer's heart and perseverance, but he's usually done himself more harm than good.

I remember a fighter who competed against one of my fighters, Bronco McKart. He was a young man with a lot of capability, but McKart simply outboxed him. After three rounds, it became apparent to the fans, the judges, and McKart that this young man was well past even the faintest glimmer of winning. He was cut, bruised, and battered, yet he kept fighting. Even McKart, who was already far ahead in points, wanted the fight to end. Everyone wanted the fight to end. Yet this boxer's corner kept him in the ring for nine rounds before throwing in the towel. That young man has yet to enter the ring again.

The person who keeps fighting in the face of hopeless odds appeals to our sense of heroism. He symbolizes romance, courage, idealism, and tragedy all wrapped up in one. He arouses pity and compassion in us when we read about him in books or see a movie about him. Unfortunately, in real life, when someone keeps fighting without hope of winning, he usually fails, whether it is in a job, a relationship, or another endeavor.

The idea is to win the war, not every single battle. The smart fighter knows that he doesn't have to win every single fight to still be considered a winner. By knowing when to throw in the towel, he has the opportunity to rethink his strategy and training and to come back stronger the second time around. So it is in your own life. Whenever you decide to quit a fight, you should do so in a way that allows you to come back stronger the next time around. To come back stronger, however, takes careful planning. You need to have a good corner who you can really trust when you need to devise a strategy for the future.

It's useful to think of the important situations in your life as you would a stock trade. Perhaps you've done all of the homework, studied the stock carefully, timed your purchase, and bought just the right number of shares. However, no sooner do you purchase the stock than it begins to fall. Day after day you watch the stock decline and your investment disappear. Despite all of your careful planning and educated decisions, the stock is losing money. The smart investor, of course, will know when to sell the stock and keep his losses to a minimum. Conversely, the stubborn investor will hold onto the stock, clinging to the belief that he is right and the stock market is wrong. He will watch his investment continue to dwindle. There's a good chance the stubborn investor will lose everything and be unable to make future investments.

In everyday life, it's often hard to know when to throw in the towel. Is a bad relationship really better than no relationship? Is the dead-end job better than taking the risk of finding another job? You are always capable of improving yourself and your situation. One of the vital ways you can move ahead is by not only recognizing opportunities when they come within reach but also by recognizing when you have become entangled in a hopeless, unwinnable battle.

Emotionally you may know when the end of a situation has come, yet you keep fighting against your better judgment. Perhaps what keeps you going is your sense of pride, or perhaps you hope that some outside intervention will occur. Yet very rarely do these situations turn around. When the situation has reached this point, you are no longer fighting to win but fighting to lose in a more spectacular manner.

A smart investor knows when to sell a stock that begins plummeting. A company knows when to discontinue a product that isn't selling. And you usually sense when a situation in your personal or professional life is hopeless. The fact is, the longer you stay in a losing situation, the more you risk. Inside the ring, fighters can risk permanent injury; outside the ring, you risk losing your most valuable resources: time and effort.

As a manager, I've occasionally had to make the decision to throw in the towel for one of my fighters. I do it by weighing the risk. Is he able to get in a punch that will end the fight? Is there a chance he'll get seriously hurt if he keeps going? In the sport of boxing, every good manager knows when the fight is over, even if the bell for the last round hasn't rung.

Fighting beyond the point where a win is possible can drag down chances for future wins. Just as an investor may take the money from a stock that is plunging and use it to buy a stock that is rising, so, too, should you value your time and effort. With nothing to possibly gain in the current battle, the smart fighter will immediately start thinking toward the future. You usually know when this moment arrives in your own mind. In boxing, it is usually the fighter's corner, not the fighter personally, who throws in the towel. In the personal sphere, unlike boxing, you have to make the decision and take the responsibility yourself. You have to set your own limits and make the tough decision to abandon an effort. Never listen to the audience. In the boxing world, the audience is always waiting in anticipation of a spectacular finish. They want the winner to win by a knockout and the loser to be defeated in the most spectacular way possible. And why not? They are bystanders without a personal attachment to the men in the ring.

You have those in your own corner and those outside that circle of intimates. People in your life who have no genuine interest in your well-being will tell you what they think you want to hear in order to avoid conflict. At other times they may even want to see you fail out of jealousy or other less-than-charitable motives. Trust your own judgment and that of the people in your corner.

As I've pointed out already, a good corner is made up of people who will help you analyze a situation and make the right decision. Just as they helped prepare you for your fight and comforted you between rounds, so, too, will they give you honest advice with your best interest in mind. In the heat of battle, your own judgment is sometimes blurred. It is in such instances that a good corner can provide an objective point of view. The audience, on the other hand, will shout from their seats anything that pops into their minds at the moment.

In the boxing ring, when you throw in the towel, the fight ends very quickly. In life, you very often have the advantage of timing your defeats. You have the ability to set both expectations and limits for any situation. For instance, suppose you are working in a dead-end job where the boss lacks any appreciation of your hard work. You've reached the end of your rope and you decide to get yourself out of the situation. The first thing you should do is to prepare yourself mentally for the change. You can start by first accepting the situation and the idea that the job is, in fact, over. Get yourself used to the idea that you no longer belong in that office, factory, or line of work, even if you are still going to work every day. Come to grips with the notion that by staying you will do yourself more harm than good. These are not easy things to think about; however, if you have good people in your corner, you can make the decision and transition much easier.

The second thing you should do is to start planning your strategy. After throwing in the towel, a fighter will start planning his strategy for the next fight almost immediately after leaving the arena. In real life, you can start planning even before you leave the ring. Begin by analyzing the situation. What was it you liked and disliked about the job? What skills did you develop? How can you build on those skills? What other firms or industries can best make use of your skills?

If you're stuck in a hopeless job and know that you have to leave it, you will be in a better position if you start looking for another job before you quit. This strategy might include performing an assignment that will gain you recognition in your field and make you more desirable to future employers. You might even begin by subtly networking within your industry, talking to others who work for firms that seem attractive to you. Or you might start training for another line of work.

What you should *not* do is storm into the boss's office and quit on the spot. Everyone has fantasies about this, but these scenarios almost never turn out very well. You should also avoid letting the quality of your work decline. Not only do you risk a knockout before you can leave on your own terms, but the shoddy work you performed during the last weeks or months on a job will be remembered long after you've left. If there is a problem at work, you should fix it before leaving. Always try to leave on terms that will make your company aware that they are losing a quality employee.

The rules for ending a relationship are similar. Set limits and reasonable expectations for yourself. Prepare yourself mentally for the relationship to end, then come up with a strategy. This might include going to the gym and getting in better shape. Perhaps you need to get a job to become more self-sufficient. Another strategy may include going back to school to learn something new, or you might want to formulate a plan to meet more interesting people. Or you may simply want to take up a hobby to fill the extra personal time you will have when the relationship ends.

I've seen many of my friends and acquaintances stay in bad relationships long beyond the time when it makes sense to leave. I've done the same thing. Most of us do. We find ourselves constantly making excuses for the other person and ignoring all the small signs that tell us the relationship is over. At the heart of this is a fear that we will never find anyone else. Even a bad relationship, we tell ourselves, is better than no relationship. Unfortunately, this thinking is a self-fulfilling prophecy because we won't find anyone better as long as we are attached to the wrong person. As soon as we leave the relationship, we immediately give ourselves more options. We can then take full advantage of the opportunities presented to us.

Okay, I know it's tough out there. I've walked the walk. Getting divorced after being married for thirty years is not easy. All the good men seem to be taken. The key word is *seem*. Appearances can be deceiving. Believe me, there are still plenty of good men around. Perhaps they're hiding in another social group or working in the kind of job with which you have no contact. They may be laying low. They may be the cousin of one of your co-workers. But they *are* out there. They're just a little harder to find these days. If you're in a miserable, tried-everything-and-can't-be-fixed relationship, throw in the towel. Only then will new doors open for you.

Moving On

The professional life of an athlete is very short compared to the lives of the rest of us. An athlete, if he is lucky, has a few precious peak years in which to secure his position in the history books and make enough money to last a lifetime. All athletes I've ever known—boxers, baseball players, and quarterbacks—are all keenly aware of this fact. It is part of what feeds their hunger to win, and to a certain extent, what pushes them to greatness. You will never hear an athlete say, "Someday I'll make that great play," or "Someday I'll have a shot at the championship." The best athletes want to make every play great. They want to go for the championship as soon as possible. In many instances, this attitude extends to all facets of their lives. They want to squeeze as much out of each day as they do out of each game. The smart ones, however, plan their careers as carefully as any business venture.

To some extent, we are all like professional athletes. Although few of us have careers that consider thirty to be near retirement age, we should look at our careers and our lives realistically at each phase. Life is like one of those moving sidewalks you ride on in airports. Fighting the natural flow will not halt the forward movement and will tire you out unnecessarily.

Every day I see middle-aged women dressing in the fashions of teenagers. These are attractive, often intelligent women, yet there is something odd about their choice of clothes. Many of these women are, in fact, stunning-looking forty- or fifty-year-olds, but their attempts to compete in fashion with twenty-year-olds often make them look ridiculous. Indeed, the contrast between their age and the type of clothes they wear is sometimes so sharp that they actually tend to look older than their age. Very simply, these women refuse to acknowledge their own reality: they are no longer twenty. And what's more, by competing with twenty-year-olds, they will invariably lose. A twenty-year-old body is not the same as a forty-year-old body, and a forty-year-old's taste is very rarely in synch with a twenty-year-old's.

They put themselves in the ring with opponents who may be at peak condition just when they themselves are slowing down. What's more, they are not using their best assets to their advantage. They are not only choosing to fight the wrong opponents but fighting on their opponents' terms. I'm not advocating a rocking chair and shawl for these women. However, my advice to them is to acknowledge and accept where you are in your own development. Feel good about who you are and what you've become. Keep fit, make yourself attractive, and above all, be yourself. You can still dress fashionably and with flair. I consider myself a rather wild, adventurous dresser. I love animal prints, fringe, and bright colors. But at the same time, I don't wear miniskirts, spandex, or bikinis. I had my turn, and now I leave those styles to the girls half my age.

I'm now in my fifties and a grandmother, and frankly, I've never felt better. I still work out, keep a schedule that would tire most twenty-year-olds, and have never felt better about myself or my career. As a member of the fifty-something generation, I know I have enough experience to work more effectively than the most hustling youngster and enough good years ahead to gain even more experience and to meet new challenges. I look at the twenty- and thirty-year-olds just starting families and think: been there, done that. So why on earth would I want to repeat it? When I was just starting out, it was an exciting challenge. Today, it's a challenge I feel I've already met and would be pointless to repeat. As a grandmother, I love visiting with my grandchildren and spoiling them with new clothes and toys, but I'm very grateful that I don't have to deal with two-in-the-morning feedings or childish tantrums.

The best part of getting older is accepting it. I surprise people all the time by openly telling my age. Many women hide their age like it was a classified government secret. I meet women all the time who shave as many as ten years off their age. They don't realize that people are looking at them and thinking, "She must have had a rough life to look so old for her age." I am proud of my age and freely offer it when asked.

I believe it was Willie Pep, one of the greatest all-time fighters, with a win record of more than 200 fights, who said something to the effect of, "The first thing a fighter loses is his legs. Then he loses his chin. And finally he loses his friends." The same can be said for life outside the ring. A person's legs are what give him drive and energy. They can be seen as the youthful exuberance and energy that propel him through the day. The chin is what allows a person to stand up to punishment, to take the hard knocks and tough shots and keep coming back at an opponent. And, friends, well, very often the leap and the chin vanish when we hit a losing streak.

As good a fighter as Pep was, he failed to see life beyond the ring. Perhaps that narrow focus is what made him great. Willie fought for twenty-six years, with a record of 229 wins, 11 losses, and 1 draw. However, he didn't see what a smart fighter gains through a lifetime of experience in and out of the ring. Yes, as we get older we may not be able to move as fast and we are more vulnerable to the blows that life deals us. However, if we learn anything from the experience gained in our youth, we should be able to compensate for diminished speed through ingenuity and adapt to the next stage in our lives.

A great fighter has two choices: he can keep climbing into the ring with younger and stronger opponents only to lose again and again, to be remembered as a has-been who ended his career with a string of humiliating defeats, or he can assess his assets and choose to build on them to launch a second career. Pep retired in 1959 but made a half-hearted and short-lived comeback in 1965. He lost his last fight to a relatively unhearalded boxer in 1966. The best fighters realize when their championship days are waning and begin planning for the next step in their careers. Naturally, they plan financially and make investments for the future, but they also begin looking around for new career paths more suitable to their abilities at this stage in life.

The most visible second careers for athletes are as spokespersons for products. These are the athletes who choose to capitalize on their fame and remain in the public eye. More common, however, are the athletes who love the sport and take jobs as trainers and coaches. Frankly, these are the athletes I most admire. They have decided to take their knowledge and love of the sport and pass it along to a new generation. They will be remembered not only as great competitors but as great trainers who helped others to win championships. It is much better to be remembered as a great athlete turned great trainer than a champion who weathered a slow and often painful decline into obscurity.

Many people confuse this transition or "moving on" with throwing in the towel. Nothing could be farther from the truth. Transitions into other areas as you grow older are the most natural things in the world. They are what allows you to keep growing, both professionally and personally.

What it takes to make the transition is a hard, honest look at yourself. You should prepare for the transition just as hard as you prepare for any other fight or challenge: assess your strengths as well as your weaknesses, and size up the opponent you intend to face. This may involve setting new goals for yourself or figuring out a way to build and utilize the skills you've learned over the years.

Perhaps the thing that makes this transition so painful is that you're not often given a choice. You certainly don't have a say in whether you get older. But you can decide along the way the things you will and won't change about yourself. However, some of the most painful examples are when you are forced to change your life suddenly. A death in the family, a divorce, and the loss of a job are all examples of the kinds of situations that force you to move on. All of these are traumatic experiences, apart from any kind of life changes they may entail.

When my husband left me, it was one of the most traumatic events of my life. It happened without warning and changed my life forever. Naturally I was upset. I would be lying to you if I said I wasn't upset, mad, and hurt. Fortunately, I had good people in my corner. My kids, friends, and relatives all rallied around me during those first few days when I was still in shock. However, after the initial shock wore off and I was able to think clearly (in good part because of the support they offered), I decided to keep moving. What choice did I have? The bottom line was, I would eventually have to go out and face the world. I would have to go back to work. Instinctively, I knew that the longer I stayed away from my work and the outside world, the harder it would be to get back into it.

It was difficult at first. For the first few days I felt as if I were just going through the motions. But day by day it became easier. I became accustomed to the idea of being single again. I decided to move to Los Angeles and start a new life. Out there were new faces, new fighters, and new challenges. After talking it over with friends and family, I decided to make the move.

I'm reminded of a friend whose husband died at a relatively young age. She had, I know, expected many more years of marriage, and his death was devastating to her. Yet she was still young. She didn't "look like a widow," and she decided, after a period of grieving, not to act like one either. She was thankful for the years she had spent with her husband and continued to cherish his memory, but she was not going to mourn him forever.

The process that she went through was gradual. She reentered life alone at her own pace. First, she cut her hair in a new style. Then she began going to the gym on a regular basis. Over the months, the transformation was remarkable. She lost weight, then had a face-lift to remove a few minor wrinkles. Finally, when she felt she was ready, she moved to a new city and a new job. She began dating again and was soon in a great relationship. When I talk to her or visit, she speaks about the years she spent with her husband fondly. Her memories of him and their life together are intact and precious to her. Yet she has managed to create a new life for herself. It wasn't easy, but those first few tentative steps eventually blossomed into a happy second life.

When another friend of mine got divorced, she began shopping at garage sales, an activity her husband always hated. It wasn't long before she discovered that she had a knack for finding valuable objects among the household clutter. She soon turned her avocation into a full-time job, searching out items at garage sales, estate sales, and auctions. The world of antiques has not only opened a whole new career path for her, but she's also met an entirely new set of friends who share her passion.

I could fill up a large volume writing about people I've known who have started over or made transitions later in life. I'm a firm believer that one thing always leads to another. The changes don't have to be traumatic or dramatic to open a whole new world filled with new people for you. However, you do have to decide in which direction you're going to travel. Sometimes you don't get much notice when a change comes in your life, but that doesn't mean you can't create a fight plan and train *after* it occurs. Moving to California was the right decision for me. However, for someone else, it might be something as simple as indulging a longtime interest in photography or art history by taking a night class or discovering a passion for a new hobby.

It's only a matter of seeing the possibilities ahead instead of looking behind at what's past. If you do this correctly, the second act of your career and personal life can complement the first part and be just as rewarding.

Sometimes we move on because we seek challenges. Unfortunately, a lot of times we are forced to move on after a divorce, the unhappy breakup of a relationship, or the death of a loved one. Here is a list of things I would recommend doing when a relationship ends, for whatever reason.

When Love Moves on

Change something about your appearance. It could be a new hairstyle, losing weight, buying new clothes, or changing your makeup. As small and superficial as these adjustments may seem, they do help overcome a heartache. They are symbolic in that they tell others as well as yourself that you are willing to accept change. And they will alter the way people perceive you, including new friends as well as old. Be radical. If you've always cursed your small breasts, get implants. Get that nose job you always wanted. Get your teeth capped.

Find a totally new hobby or social outlet. It doesn't matter if it's ballroom dancing or karate, take that course you always wanted to take. You'll not only meet new people but learn a skill that occupies your mind and your time.

Join a club or civic organization. Fulfill your dream of acting with a local theater company or join a grass-roots political group. Participating in these organizations will lead you to new people and open new doors for you both socially and mentally.

Redecorate your home. Whether you hire an army of contractors to tear down walls to build a palace, plan a do-it-yourself paint job in the bedroom, or simply rearrange the furniture, the changes—even minor ones—will show your acceptance of starting over. And they will also help you accept the larger changes in your life.

Volunteer for a good cause. This will not only make you feel better, you'll be helping people in the process. I became involved in a shelter for battered and abused women, and it is now a regular part of my life. I also do work with Special Olympics and the Muscular Dystrophy Association.

Do something totally out of character. You know you've always wanted that Porsche. Now's the time to buy it if you can afford it. It doesn't have to be that outrageously expensive, the point is to do *something*—just make sure it's safe. One-night stands and doing drugs definitely don't qualify. What qualifies is signing up for an open-mike talent contest or belting out a full-volume rendition of "I Will Survive" at a karaoke bar to shock your friends. Take up yoga, painting, or knitting. Become a foster parent, adopt a pet from the Humane Society, or rent out a room in your home.

ROUND

11

THERE AIN'T GONNA BE NO REMATCH

When Sylvester Stallone's Rocky character stood battered, bloody, and exhausted, but still undefeated at the end of the movie, he uttered the line, "There ain't gonna be no rematch." Truer words were never uttered. Rocky had reached his goal by paying the price inside and outside the ring. He trained hard, formulated his fight plan, and fought with tons of heart. All of this carried him through the fight. He had accomplished what he set out to do—and more. Having paid the price, he told the world that he didn't need to prove himself again. Not at the same task, anyway.

In our own lives, we often forget these lessons. Part of this has to do with the goals we set for ourselves. We accomplish the most arduous tasks and receive acclaim for it, but rather than move on to new goals, we keep repeating the same successes. That is just a fact of business life. Secretaries are expected to type perfect letters again and again. Paperwork has to be filled out correctly time after time. The hairstyle we've given to a regular customer should always be as perfect as possible. These are the day-to-day challenges we should all take pride in accomplishing to the best of our ability.

However, even as we continue to meet our everyday objectives, we should continue to set new and higher goals for ourselves. Perhaps these are long-term personal goals or business goals, but it is still important to work toward higher objectives. Only by meeting these goals do we grow, both professionally and personally. The salesperson who lands the million-dollar account should set his sights higher, perhaps aiming toward the two-million-dollar mark or trying to land accounts in new territory. There is absolutely no sense in resting on our laurels. We live in a competitive world, and yesterday's winners are very often surpassed by today's up-and-comers. This can often be a difficult task. After all, there is always the chance of failure, and that's scary. However, there is no greater failure than people who don't push themselves, in a smart way, toward the next goal or level.

There are fighters who have 25–0 records, but we've never heard of them—and most likely never will—because they're not champions. They only fight opponents they know they can defeat. They fight the weak and the untalented. They win again and again, fighting essentially the same fight over and over. Their fights are boring, and as athletes, they never develop to their full potential. They might have a lot of natural talent but never develop it because they never have to stretch themselves. Eventually, they may even lose their heart or lower the quality of their training. In boxing, as in any of life's arenas, boxers are only as good as the challenges they take on. They have a long string of victories, but they will never make it to the big time if they're not tested.

Conversely, a fighter may have an 18–3 record, but it's a better record if those three defeats were championship fights. These are fighters who are looking to build on their wins and progress. Anyone knowledgeable in the fight game knows to look beyond the win-loss record. The same is true in our personal and business lives.

Whenever I hire someone, I always look at his or her resumé. Perhaps someone was a secretary for ten years. I look at the responsibilities she held at each job. If the responsibilities were the same throughout her career—typing, filing, answering phones—then I know she isn't a winner. If, however, I see that her responsibilities grew with each job, then I know I have someone with spark and initiative.

The same is true for other positions. Who would you rather hire, the sales manager with ten years of experience who started out as assistant sales manager, or the person who started as a secretary and worked her way up to sales manager? The person who is building on her skills is truly a winner. She is most likely the one who will possess the heart, talent, and drive to succeed at just about any goal she sets her mind on. The person who has built on her wins is, not surprisingly, the person who has mastered the art of training, strategy, and getting the right people in her corner. She is the one who formulates fight plans and sticks with them. She is a winner with a future.

We also defeat ourselves by taking on needless rematches

because of our egos. A fighter who emerges from the ring having just barely won the title would be foolish to return any time in the near future to face the same opponent again. Perhaps the odds were against him from the start and he triumphed in spite of that. Instead of acting cocky and thinking himself invincible, he should honestly acknowledge how close he came to defeat and set about preparing himself for the next challenge.

I've seen smart, capable businesspeople snatch defeat from the jaws of victory by thinking that the high-risk move that succeeded today will work equally well tomorrow. After every close call, real winners take time to honestly evaluate the win. Was it pure luck? And if it was, why didn't the fight plan work? Every win, especially the close ones, require scrutiny. Luck is fickle, as they say, and people who rely on sheer luck are bound to fall hard.

Most people learn from their mistakes. After all, when we lose, either in business or love, we can most often see exactly what we did wrong. When we win, we often do a whole host of things right. However, we should in no way confuse a win by the smallest of margins for a clear victory. We should, of course, accept the victory gracefully as a true winner would. But we should also examine the win closely. If we made mistakes, then we should accept them and seek to rectify them. A narrow win affords us a sterling opportunity. Not only do we get the satisfaction of winning but the chance to reevaluate and improve ourselves for the next bout.

There's an old saying: "A man can't cross the same river twice." This is because the water that he swam the first time has already moved beyond the point where he crossed. Even if he ran to catch up to the water, he would be at a different position on the river. Life involves change, like the river. A man can't cross the same river twice, and a fighter can't fight the same fight twice. His opponent has changed either through training or lack of it, and the fighter has changed for the same reasons. The changes may be for the better or worse, but there are literally thousands of variables over which the fighter has no control. His opponent may have a new trainer or manager. The opponent may have simply begun to take the sport more seriously and put in longer hours training. Or the ref may be more inclined toward the other fighter. All of these things are why no smart fighter—no champion—ever takes the prospect of a rematch lightly.

The same is true for each one of us. The client who bought your product so easily last year may have had a financial setback that makes him a tougher customer this year. The woman who was so pleased with the hairstyle you gave her just a few weeks ago might now be a tough critic if someone made a harsh remark about her hair. Every situation is not the same as the one before. There are elements in every rematch that are beyond your control. Your only protection is to keep seeking to improve yourself and not to allow yourself to become lazy or inattentive because you've "been there and done that" once or twice before. Just as fighters can grow cocky when they face an opponent they've already defeated, so, too, can you grow arrogant in your everyday tasks. And then, when an unexpected element catches you by surprise, you are left confused, or worse, down for the count.

There are also some cases in which you really should quit while you're ahead. This is often as difficult as setting your sights on the next challenge. After all, you won. Why shouldn't you get back into the ring? One reason: you could lose and lose badly. For example, if you're a woman who has just removed herself from an unpleasant or destructive relationship, you would be foolish to become involved with the same type of man all over again. You've managed to escape with your self-respect and without investing an abundance of time or money in the man. Why on earth would you go back to either him or someone similar? If you're driving down the street and lose control on a patch of ice and only by sheer luck avoid a head-on collision, you would be foolish to immediately drive around the block and go over that same patch of ice again. Having been down that street, you've experienced first-hand that it only offers disaster.

When we think of rematches, we immediately think of the loser. We think of someone who receives a second chance at victory. Every rematch, almost without exception, is an opportunity for the fighter who has been defeated. As winners, we often have very little to gain by repeating fights. If we win, then it confirms what should already be known: that we were up to the task. However, if we lose, not only do we lose the last fight, but the previous win is also somewhat tarnished.

Smart fighters choose their matches with great care, and nowhere is this more important than in deciding on whether to take on a rematch. Winners decide if there is going to be a rematch. They have control of the situation. Many times they don't even know that with their victory comes the decision of whether to "do it again." That's a shame because one of the most valuable benefits of winning is having that decision-making power.

At other times people don't even realize they've won. For instance, after getting out of a bad relationship, many women I know feel as if they have failed. Nonsense. They haven't failed; they've escaped—and by escaping, they've won. But instead of high-fiving the people in their corner, they mope and shuffle back to the locker room. Wrong attitude. They're out of the relationship with a whole world of choices in front of them. They should take time to celebrate and then make the right choices. Remember, *losers always scream for a rematch. Winners don't need one.*

Never Consider Doing It Again When . . .

The fight was a no-win situation. You've finally escaped an impossible situation. That emotionally unhealthy relationship has just ended, and the person begs and pleads for you to take him or her back. If nothing substantial has changed, then the second time around will probably be exactly like the first time, perhaps worse. The same holds true for jobs. If a job at a particular company was horrible the first time, chances are it will be just as bad the next.

Your success was dependent wholly on your corner. For example, you only made an impossible deadline on a major project because the people in your corner pitched in to help at the last minute. You should count on your corner, but not to a degree where they fight the fight for you.

Luck was on your side. A rare piece of luck or coincidence was instrumental in helping you accomplish your goal. Yes, luck sometimes does happen just when you need it most. You should appreciate it and want it but never, ever count on it. Luck is a very fickle friend.

You were saved by the bell. A last-second intervention by a boss or a loved one saved you from attempting an impossible task at which you would surely have failed. If the task in front of you was absolutely impossible the first time, chances are not much will have changed—except your luck—the second time you attempt it.

The other guy beat himself. Your success was wholly dependent on another's inability or lack of preparation. If you depend on your opponent's lack of action, you are setting yourself up for a major defeat.

The win remains a mystery. When you don't know exactly why you succeeded, it is very unlikely you can repeat the win again. You have to be absolutely honest with yourself in assessing each victory.

WINNER AND STILL CHAMPION!

When the final bell rings, the words every fighter listens for is an "Winner and still champion!" or "Winner and *new* champion!" It is the final affirmation heard above the roar of the crowd that all of his hard work has finally paid off. They are the words that make the victory official. The announcement means that the fighter has reached the top of his profession: he fought a good, clean fight and came out on top. It means that he trained hard, built his strategy well, and skillfully followed a fight plan that was well thought out in advance. He not only possessed what it took to be a champ but used and honed those attributes in a way that truly made him a champ.

But is winning really everything? In a word, yes. We humans are competitive creatures, whether we like to admit it or not. Even if we are just competing against our own personal best, the thrill of accomplishment and reaching a goal is one of the strongest feelings we can have. However, winning does not mean making truckloads of money, unless that is how you personally define winning. Nor does it mean fame or notoriety. It is up to each of us, as individuals, to write our own definition of a winner and then set about going for the title.

I know many, many winners outside of the sports world. Some are doctors, lawyers, and accountants. Some own small businesses and are always struggling to make ends meet. Yet in their own way, they are all champs. Perhaps they will never see their names up in lights above a sold-out arena. They may never hear a crowd roaring for their victory. But that's the way it is for most of us. They nevertheless get that final affirmation of accomplishment from a boss, a friend, or a loved one. It is just as sweet and inspiring as if it were shouted over a loudspeaker in a crowded arena. There may not be refs around to hold our arms up in victory, but those in our corner—husbands, wives, lovers, or friends—will know.

We should also remember those who helped us reach that achievement. Whether it's a championship bout or a small win, no fighter wins entirely on his own. He got there with the help of his corner, and the best fighters recognize that fact. They also recognize the fact that they faced a worthy opponent who probably fought as hard as possible.

So often after a win we forget to acknowledge those who helped us achieve our goal. We've all seen Academy Award winners thank the people who made their success possible. Very rarely in our own lives, however, do we get the opportunity to make a speech on prime-time television. Remember, even those small victories count. Here are just a few of the ways I've found to thank the people who have helped me along the way.

Give Credit Where Credit Is Due

A personal note. Sometimes just saying "thank you" isn't enough. Often a brief note expressing your sincere thanks will let that person know that you were genuinely grateful for his or her help. Even an e-mail can make your feelings known. The key is expressing your gratitude and appreciation in a tangible way.

Dinner. I've seen this time and again in the business world. The smart boss will thank his staff by taking them out to a nice dinner. Not only is it a real morale booster, but it builds a sense of team spirit among the different staff members. However, you don't need a fancy restaurant to show your appreciation for someone's help. Cooking a special dinner for the family or a loved one can be even more meaningful. Or if dinner is beyond your budget, how about a nice lunch? Or a drink?

A gift. Flowers are almost always appreciated by women, but there are times when they are just inappropriate. In those instances, a small but tasteful gift is the right thing—a book, a gift certificate, a CD. For men, a key chain, a bottle of wine, a book, or a DVD make a nice gift.

Public acknowledgment. Although we often don't get to make speeches, we can and should acknowledge those who contributed to our success. I was in an office not long ago where a vice president praised his staff for a job well done while in a meeting with the division head. The staff, of course, was present. The acknowledgment not only made his staff look good but made the vice president look as if he had assembled a winning team, which he had.

This may all seem very basic, but in the excitement of accomplishment it is easy to forget to offer credit to those who helped you achieve your goal. It is also easy to overlook small achievements, which also deserve recognition. If you look back over each day or week of your life, you see many different outcomes, both wins and losses. Some of them are important, others are unimportant. But you should acknowledge every win and thank the people who helped you to make it possible.

There are two opposing views on competition. One saying is, "It doesn't matter if you win or lose, it's how you play the game." The other old saying goes, "If it doesn't matter if you win or lose, then why keep score?" Which theory do you subscribe to? I believe they are both true in a way, and depending on the situation, either one may apply.

Winners

When I think of winners, I think of hundreds of people I've known both in and out of the fight business. I know travel agents, actors, doctors, lawyers, and cops whom I consider true champions. They all have certain traits, which I have distilled into the following guidelines.

Plan ahead for success. Very few winners are surprised by their success. They've worked hard and know they deserve it. Looking back on their achievements, they can tell you exactly what they did to reach their goals.

Don't always give in. If you believe in something strongly, then stand up for it.

Don't go along with other people's plans just to be liked or accepted. Give your honest opinions when asked.

Don't be taken for granted. If there are signs that you are being taken for granted at work or in a relationship, do something about it. Make yourself noticed.

Don't dwell on the worst-case scenario. Be aware of it, but if you expect the worst in every situation, then very often it becomes a self-fulfilling prophesy.

Don't disparage yourself. If you're ten pounds overweight, then plan on losing those ten pounds. Work on those things that can be fixed, and don't dwell on those that can't be changed. Don't continually tell people how fat you are.

Don't ignore negative comments about yourself. If someone is talking behind your back at work or in your circle of friends, then let him know that his comments have gotten back to you and that you don't appreciate it. Hit the problem squarely in the face.

Don't accept bad service. If there is a problem with service, then reflect that problem in the tip or point out politely, yet firmly, the kind of service you expect. Don't just sit there and be a victim.

Never accept emotional or physical abuse. A winner will seek help to fix the situation. Do not allow yourself to be treated in a degrading fashion.

Don't let people take advantage of you. Real friends know when enough is enough and what is too much. This is more than just having your best interests at heart. It is a genuine empathy.

In our lives, we should not just strive to win, but to win in ways that allow us to be proud of our victories. We all have it in ourselves to be champions, if not in the ring or on the playing field, then in our jobs and with our families. It is there, in our offices and homes, that we can strive for a greatness that really is within reach. There may not be the applause, cheers, or the million-dollar salary, but there is the opportunity to be a superstar to our friends, our coworkers, and our families.

Index